D0990879

HENRY THOREAU
THE COSMIC
YANKEE

HENRY THOREAU,

THE COSMIC YANKEE

By

J. BROOKS ATKINSON

ALFRED A. KNOPF

New York 1927

Copyright 1927

BY *ALFRED A. KNOPF, INC.*

Manufactured in the United States
of America

CONTENTS

Chapter One
Page 1
BEAUTY FROM A SERENE MIND

Chapter Two
Page 28
SPEAKING A GOOD WORD FOR THE TRUTH

Chapter Three
Page 45
"HENRY IS—WITH DIFFICULTY—SWEET"

Chapter Four
Page 72
STRANGE VERSE AND PLAIN PROSE

Chapter Five
Page 99
WALDEN

Chapter Six
Page 127
GLEANINGS FROM THE FIELD

Chapter Seven
Page 140
"A MAN OF IDEAS AND PRINCIPLES"

THE FRONTISPIECE
is cut in wood by
PERCY SMITH

From the Ricketson Medallion used
by permission of

Houghton Mifflin
Company

HENRY THOREAU

THE COSMIC
YANKEE

CHAPTER ONE

BEAUTY FROM A SERENE MIND

Now that Henry David Thoreau has come into his heritage as the interpreter of nature, great in thought and sublime in perception, it is more difficult than ever to understand him as a man among men and to grasp the immediate value of his thought for a new period in American culture. Of his inner life we have ample evidence in the magic words he wrote; he was a mystic full of divine wisdom. Wonder and beauty came to him from remote sources beyond our concrete world; and he, more than any other writer on nature, has transmitted these precious elements without smudging them with egregious phrases. But about his life in the streets of Concord, as a villager among his townspeople, the information is untrustworthy and contradictory. All the sources are poisoned with good intentions.

Excepting Emerson's all too brief memorial address, we have not a single reliable, full-

length portrait of him from his contemporaries. His growing fame after his death put
a premium upon idealizing him as a human
being; and those who did not impatiently dismiss him as a freak painted him as a genial
comrade, jocund in the field. What could be
more wretchedly misleading? W. E. Channing, his closest friend, was admittedly a de-
fender. Frank Sanborn and Edward Emerson, son of the great Concord sage, lacked the
force to report fully a protean philosopher
who denied in social life all the amenities they
accepted as final. The friendliest interpreta-
tions persisted in defending what he arrogantly dismissed as trivial. "You may rely
on it," he wrote to a distant correspondent,
"that you have the best of me in my books,
and that I am not worth seeing personally, the
stuttering, blundering clod-hopper that I am.
Even poetry, you know, is in one sense an infinite brag and exaggeration." Discounting
the natural modesty in that manifesto of character, I believe it to be a truer description of
himself—of his dual nature—than the truc-
ulent pages of Sanborn, the turgid phrases of
Channing, or the classical panegyric of Edward Emerson. No matter how highly we
may esteem Thoreau as a herald of the mil-

lennium, or how closely we may come to the radiance of his thought, I am sure most of us would have found him a refractory person. He could be no less forbidding as a person than he was alluring in his written, mystic dreams.

The fact is that the next generation in America had no conception of transcendental thought—less than we have in this slowly revitalizing era. After the Civil War materialism pushed all the dreamers off their hilltops; industrial expansion drained the sources of humanistic thought. Nothing, I think, is more astounding than the completeness of that subjugation, by which Emersonian and Thoreauvian thought was swept impetuously aside; even Whitman, who lingered on, began to burn less fiercely. Although those three men gave us our first consciousness of identity as a country rich in human resources, and although they held out the promise of a full, healthy, independent life with roots sent down into a sweet and fecund soil, their cultural descendants were content with scratching the surface. Independence, hope, passion were dust in their mouths. They lacked, not only sympathy, but understanding. This is why we must depend almost exclusively upon the journals and the formal writings of these visionary prophets for our images of them as men.

In fine, what the next generation lacked completely was the precise Americanism that Thoreau and Emerson had eagerly pulled from our soil. In a generation of critics and biographers who were first of all placid gentlemen, reassured by their own formalism and sentimentality, the evanescent dreams of Thoreau were patronizingly set down as charming. Lowell was injudicious enough to attack him; but that was at least an honest expression of his code of values. Those who were by natural sympathy on Thoreau's side seem to me to have made a worse muddle of their judgments. Under the spell of the literary mellowness of their good nature, and their spurious lore of Horace and Virgil, this tight-lipped, passionate American seeker after his own soul became a sort of elf of the woods— an ineffable social aberration. "Surely a True Thomas of Ercildoune returned from his stay in Faërie with its queen's gift of a 'tongue that shall never lie'," says Edward Waldo Emerson. "This young Theophrastus or La Bruyère," says the pontifical Frank Sanborn, sole custodian of Henry Thoreau. Indeed, as the years went on, Sanborn gathered up Thoreau

so much to himself that in the last edition of
his biography he took the supreme liberty of
editing "the rough and unpolished sentences
of the Journals, letters, etc." Thus he spared
Thoreau the humiliation of Thoreau!

For the present period, which is becoming
ever more conscious of itself, the value of
Thoreau is not his resemblance to cultured
men, but his difference. Somehow in the be-
wildering haste of our breathless development
we have lost sight of our origins and inheritance, and we have come to value everything
for its resemblances. We are regimented. We
read the books that are read, see the plays that
are seen; we work in offices and play on the
links amid crowds of our fellows. We fortify
ourselves against boredom with things. When
we find ourselves alone, we are terrified lest
we miss something important. Even our revo-
lutions we accomplish in the same fashion:
we make a cult of the "different," so that it
all comes round to the same thing at last. Size
fills us with a stupid awe; accumulation fills
us with envy. Records must be broken every
year. Then we divide our stock and begin
more aggressively than ever. What is the
end? Why, more of the same. As Thoreau

said of his neighbors who wanted to sell their houses in the outskirts and move into the village: "Only death will set them free."

Against all this footless hurry Thoreau set up the ideal of the enjoyment of life. Yes, he was a radical. He liked to feel himself, not an amorphous globule in a foamy maelstrom, but a free human being, related to the heroes of the past and walking properly oriented in the direction of the future. He was conscious of the divinity in life. He was as nearly free as anyone can be. Panics, disasters, catastrophes, upset those who had put all their wealth in high risks for uncertain returns. Having invested in the faculties and equipment with which life had endowed him, he remained serene. As it happened, he chose to search in nature for the securities he prized most highly, and, being a pioneer, he was in many respects fanatical. Many human qualities that we hold dear he undervalued. But he understood that the beauties of life were to be found wherever fortune had placed us, and always within ourselves. "Such is beauty ever," he wrote, "neither here nor there, now nor then, neither in Rome nor in Athens, but wherever there is a soul to admire it. If I seek her elsewhere because I do not find her at home, my search will be a fruitless one." So simple and obvious are his fundamental truths that they roar like rebellion in a complex civilization.

Between what he wrote and what he appeared to be there was a lack of harmony difficult to reconcile with his heroic being. I suppose that is why those who approach him from external accounts of his life are repelled by a look of austerity in his face. That look is not in his eyes. Even that last photograph, with its shaggy beard and rigid pose, discloses the melting beauty of his eyes; and reading his books we may depend upon it that we are penetrating Thoreau through his eyes, and that, thus, we are vouchsafed the loveliest qualities in his being. Since his Journals were not published until after his death, few of his neighbors had the chance to read him at his best. It is no wonder that, judging him by his defiant exterior, they dismissed him as an intellectual snob, who was very clumsy and socially inept into the bargain. They never knew what poetic fires burned within. Of his neighbors who did know, only Emerson, I think, had the genius to explain Thoreau's divinity.

The notion that he was an eccentric, a sour

hermit whose philosophy has no pertinence
for worldly wisemen, comes from accenting
the crudity of his exterior. On the contrary,
the essence of his thinking was never more apt
than it is now. Most of us are "instrumen-
talists" today in our living, whatever our private dogma may be. With the development of
machinery, we have come to pride ourselves
upon efficient modes of living, upon the
dynamic quality of our thinking and acting,
upon accuracy and speed. "We must be very
active," said Thoreau, "if we would be clean,
live our own life and not a languishing and
scurvy one." Thoreau loved practicability
also; he loved to have things done well, with
skill and dispatch; he despised slovenly
methods of procedure. He believed in success. Like moderns, he loved progress and
growth. The steam locomotive, rattling past
Walden Pond, set him dreaming of the glorious adventure of commerce by which the
world was pulled close together. How he
loved to smell the spices at Long Wharf in
Boston and to gaze far down the Harbor,
where the ships put out for foreign ports! The
practical development of transportation and
barter, now marvellously perfected, seemed
good to him also. *Walden* is full of such

poetry. He liked to think of himself as a practical man who gave full measure and drove a sharp bargain in his own affairs. "Who will not confess that the necessity to get money has not helped to ripen some of his schemes?" He hated stupidity, cowardice, and laziness. In general the structure of modern commercial life, I am sure, would not in itself fill him with disdain.

Above instrumentalism, however, above practicability and machine manufacturing, he esteemed the guiding motive and the flowering of the individual. "The lecturer is wont to describe the nineteenth century, the American of the last generation, in an offhand and triumphant strain, wafting him to paradise, spreading his fame by steel and telegraph, recounting the number of wooden stopples he has whittled. But he does not perceive that this is not a sincere or pertinent account of any man or nation's life. It is the hip-hip-hurrah and mutual admiration society style. Cars go by and we know their substance as well as their shadow! They stop and we get into them. But those sublime thoughts, passing on high, do not stop, and we never get into them. Their conductor is not like one of us." To Thoreau the true harvest of any enterprise was the divination of the individual as a sovereign being far more noble than the tools of his trade. If the machines do not actually release us from drudgery to the true freedom of life, if we are not happier men with finer capacities, we have missed the point completely. If we are not always more exalted than the means of our living, then we are the slaves whom Thoreau despised—saddled with farms, oppressed with mortgages, the unburied dead, whose every motion seems futile and ghastly. What is the motive? "The true laborer is recompensed by his labor, not by his employer. Industry is its own wage. Let us not suffer our hands to lose one jot of their handiness by looking behind to a mere recompense, knowing that our true endeavor cannot be thwarted, nor we be cheated of our earnings unless by not earning them. . . . When in rare moments we strive wholly with one consent, which we call a yearning, we may hope that our work will stand in an artist's gallery." Let there be an adventure, a glamour, a gusto, a blossoming of the soul, in everything that we do.

Thus the spirit of Thoreau's philosophy does not seem to me remote, unsympathetic, or impracticable; but vividly alive. Now that we are recovering from a half-century debauch of materialism and are beginning to look about us to see exactly what we have left, I am sure Thoreau would applaud our freshness, our frankness, our direct point of view, our impatience with the old shibboleths, and our determination to begin a new world. If, in the course of time, we reconcile our instrumentalism with the individual man, if we reclaim the individual from the jumble of material living and discover the true sources of happiness, inevitably we shall go to Thoreau for the vision. "You cannot perceive beauty but with a serene mind." When his was serene, he saw the potential beauties of America.

Although this book is devoted to Thoreau's thought, poetry, and character—his cosmic Yankeeism—a brief chronicle of the chief facts in his life history may serve as a helpful preliminary. Regarded as a unit, Thoreau's life had almost perfect form; it was unmistakably the well-molded product of fine art in living. Only three incidents seem to me out of character. For two or three years after graduation from Harvard College, he kept school in Concord; when he was twenty-six, he tutored Judge Emerson's children on Staten Island, N. Y. Again, when his health was

failing rapidly, at the age of forty-four he
travelled west to Minnesota in a vain endeavor to recover his strength. Otherwise,
throughout his forty-five years, he did nothing
that was not "in character," nothing that did
not coincide with the principles expressed in
his writings. One of his closest companions
observed: "His personality is in a striking degree single, he being ever the same man in his
conversation, letters, books, and the details of
his life." Thoreau's life had a sort of dramatic
unity; it revealed the precise "simplicity" that
he fiercely recommended to his neighbors.

The main root of its unity, of course, was
its environment, Concord, where he was born
in 1817 and died in 1862. His grandfather, a
younger son in a well-to-do Jersey family of
French extraction, had emigrated from St.
Helier to Boston in 1773, married a Scotch
wife, developed a profitable business in Boston, and died in Concord in 1801. Thoreau's
father settled down in Concord after failing
in business and losing most of his inherited
property. As a pencil-maker, never pros-
perous and often quite impoverished, he was
known as a quiet, honest, undistinguished villager. His wife, Cynthia Dunbar, was quick-
witted, humorous, animated, and notoriously

talkative. She came from a family that, by choosing the wrong side in the American Revolution, had lost nearly all its extensive farm properties in New England. Henry David Thoreau (or David Henry, as he was christened) was the third of four children; Helen and John were older, Sophia younger. John died in early manhood; Helen died at the age of thirty-seven. Sophia and her mother survived Henry.

Although Thoreau always maintained that beauty was to be found wherever one might happen to be, he could not have denied that fortune had been especially generous to him, that Concord was uncommonly beautiful, and that his "genius for staying at home" accordingly resulted in giving him a sustaining and varied natural background. Just where Concord leaves off and Thoreau begins is hard to define; their respective lives, human and natural, are fused into one being. Today Concord still retains its character as a New England town, richly endowed with natural beauty and historical associations. Despite a certain vanity, an indigenous sense of superiority, Concord remains one of the loveliest and most enjoyable towns in New England, with a clearly defined character. Tourists rattle through in lumbering motor-buses; the aliens have slipped in by the back way. But Concord does not yield in beauty or dignity; indeed, perhaps it is now more sententiously Concord than it was when Thoreau lived there. If he did nothing else, he defined Concord in all its parts and brought it into focus.

Hundreds of New England towns are quite as lavishly endowed with fields, woods, and gentle hills. But few are also graced with two rivers, placid or swift according to the season, and with several small ponds in the outskirts or just over the line in neighboring townships. What opportunities they gave Thoreau for sailing, for bathing and skating, and for variety in natural lore! There is nothing astounding about these properties; they are not spectacular in any respect. Rather are they gentle and ingratiating, homelike in every instance. To saunter through Concord today is to marvel at the fullness of her expression through Thoreau. He did not merely describe the country and the village and record the facts of the native phenomena. Beyond all that, his spirit was the spirit of Concord; he gave out Concord with every breath; he lived Concord.

Not that the Thoreaus enjoyed any special

prestige in Concord society, where the demar-
cations were always understood, though never
disagreeable. They were respected as honest
townsfolk; but they lived closely around the
domestic hearth and took no more prominent
part in town life than most industrious, earnest, and intelligent Concordians. In 1833, at
the age of sixteen, Thoreau was sent to Harvard College, where he was maintained
through the economy of his aunts and his elder
sister, then a school-teacher, and his own
efforts. Shy, reserved, and laconical, he slipped
through the four years without leaving any
glamorous impression upon his college mates.
One of his class-mates, Rev. John Weiss, re-
called him in the following paragraphs written
in 1865: "He was cold and unimpressible.
The touch of his hand was moist and indiffer-
ent, as if he had taken up something when he
saw your hand coming, and caught your grasp
upon it. How the prominent gray-blue eyes
seemed to rove down the path, just in advance
of his feet, as his grave Indian stride carried
him down to University Hall! He did not
care for people; his class-mates seemed very
remote. This reverie hung always about him,
and not so loosely as the odd garments which
the pious household care furnished. Thought

had not yet awakened his countenance; it was serene, but rather dull, rather plodding. The lips were not yet firm; there was almost a look of smug satisfaction lurking round their corners. It is plain now that he was preparing to hold his future views with great setness and personal appreciation of their importance. The nose was prominent, but its curve fell forward without firmness over the upper lip, and we remember him as looking very much like some Egyptian sculptures of faces, large-featured, but brooding, immobile, fixed in a mystic egoism. Yet his eyes were sometimes searching as if he had dropped, or expected to find, something. In fact his eyes seldom left the ground, even in his most earnest conversations with you.

"He would smile to hear the word 'collegiate career' applied to the reserve and inaptness of his college life. He was not signalized by the plentiful distribution of the parts and honors which fall to the successful student. Of his private tastes there is little of consequence to recall, except that he was devoted to the old English literature, and had read a good many volumes of the poetry from Gower and Chaucer down through the era of Elizabeth. In this mine he worked with quiet enthusiasm." Probably he was not well liked; he seems to have dropped out of class life completely as soon as he left college.

For two or three years after he was graduated, Thoreau obediently looked about for steady employment. He quickly abandoned teaching in the Concord grammar school when the discipline demanded by the school committee violated his sense of personal ethics. Chiefly through the enterprise of John, the two Thoreau brothers opened a very popular and successful private school for boys in 1838. It seems to have been the forerunner of the schools in which discipline is maintained by mutual consent rather than by force, in which teachers and students associate indoors and out on terms of intimacy, and in which woodland strolls are considered a legitimate part of the instruction. Although Henry performed his duties faithfully, John was the obvious animating force in the school. In 1841, when John's health began to fail, the school was closed amid genuine regrets from both parents and students. John died of lockjaw during the winter. After that Henry definitely turned toward Nature for his chief companionship; from this time on his profession was that of "saunterer." He determined to devote at least three or four hours in every day to walking; in the evening he wrote out his discoveries and his meditations in the Journals. He now became the "bachelor of Nature," in Emerson's felicitous phrase.

Of the remaining twenty-two years of his life there is little to record that does not find complete expression in his writings. In 1841 he went to live in the Emerson household. "He is to have his board, etc., for what labor he chooses to do," Emerson wrote, "and he is thus far a great benefactor and physician to me, for he is an indefatigable and skilful laborer." He wrote for the *Dial,* without stipend, and dove into the mighty swell of Transcendentalism that was then rolling through England and America. He came to know Margaret Fuller, Bronson Alcott, Ellery Channing, and his somber neighbor Nathaniel Hawthorne. While tutoring at Staten Island in 1843, he met Horace Greeley, George Ripley, Henry James, Edward Palmer, and others. He wrote haltingly for several magazines, none of which sought him out as a contributor.

In 1845 he built his hut at Walden Pond, where he lived two years and two months, "watching the progress of the seasons." That was the heyday, you will remember, of transcendental experiments in meditative living—Fruitlands and Brook Farm in particular. How the idea of the Walden retreat came to Thoreau we do not fully know. As a child, he had always wanted to live there; he had fished, bathed, and boated in Walden waters all during his boyhood. Moreover, one of his boyhood and college cronies, Stearns Wheeler, had lived in a hut on Flint's Pond in 1841, and Thoreau's Journal of that year expressed the hope that he, too, might live in a hut, but at Walden, and "hear only the wind whispering among the reeds." In his twenty-eighth year Thoreau put his scheme into practice, and lived there richly, as *Walden* testifies, until he believed that he had sucked the adventure dry. Then he returned without ceremony to the village, because it seemed to him that he "had several more lives to live, and could not spare any more time for that one." While he was at the pond, he collected the material for his most famous book, and he also completed *A Week on the Concord and Merrimac Rivers,* a gloriously elaborated, incoherent chronicle of a boating trip made with

John in 1839. *A Week* was a lamentable and
costly publishing failure.

Returning to village life, Thoreau settled
down to his chosen profession with more determination than ever and became a familiar,
lonely, brooding figure on the outskirts or
along the rivers. To support himself as his
frugal needs required he worked at carpentry
and masonry, or at surveying, or helped with
the family pencil-making. When his father
died, he devoted himself to the support of his
mother and sister in that moderately profitable industry. Sometimes he lectured, though
unsuccessfully. Frequently he made long excursions to Wachusett, Monadnock, the White
Mountains, Cape Cod, or the Maine woods.
Once he journeyed to Canada on the same
vague business. He thriftily managed the
Concord Lyceum of winter lectures, and spoke
there himself several times; but he took no
part in other social activities. He withdrew
from the local church early in his manhood.
He refused to pay a poll tax to a government
that tolerated slavery. In 1859 Thoreau suddenly amazed everyone who knew him by
championing John Brown, who had just been
arrested at Harper's Ferry. Although the
cautious townsmen counselled discretion and

earnestly advised against public meeting, Thoreau addressed a large gathering in passionate tones in the Town Hall and delivered his red-hot address again in Boston a few days later. "This exciting theme," said the *Liberator*, "seemed to have awakened 'the hermit of Concord' from his usual state of philosophic indifference and he spoke with real enthusiasm for an hour and a half. A very large audience listened to this lecture, crowding the hall half an hour before the time of its commencement, and giving hearty applause to some of the most energetic expressions of the speaker."

In 1860 Thoreau took a severe cold in the woods. Consumption set in actively. Like his grandfather, brother, and one sister, he quickly fell heir to this insidious disease. During the last years of Thoreau's life the Civil War broke out and settled down to a long, bitter contest. The misfortunes of the North in the first months filled Thoreau with anxiety; he told his friends that he could never recover while the war continued. As long as his strength lasted, and with the assistance of Sophia, he insisted upon putting his papers in order; he prepared several magazine articles solicited by the *Atlantic Monthly*

and published posthumously; he left his few
effects in good order. The end came on a
beautiful spring morning, May 6, 1862, while
Concord was warm and fragrant with the new
season. He lies buried in the Sleepy Hollow
cemetery in Concord.

Of romance and affection in the usual sense
of the words there seems to have been none in
Thoreau's nature. Sentimental folk insist,
upon the flimsiest evidence, that he fell in love
with Ellen Sewall in his early twenties. Her
brother attended the Thoreaus' school. She
frequently visited with the Thoreau brothers
and sisters when she was staying with relatives
in Concord. According to the sentimental
falderal, John loved her, too; and Henry,
magnanimous as the devil, stepped aside when
she showed her preference for John. The
"gentle boy" celebrated in Henry's poem entitled "Sympathy" is said, on Emerson's authority, to have been Ellen Sewall. However,
Ellen never expressed herself on this strange,
sentimental interlude, although she had time
enough, if she had wanted to, in the years after
Thoreau's death. Like a thousand other romantic young maidens she settled down to a
comfortable married life with some less distinguished partner, and slumped into medioc-

rity. Most of this incident rests upon pure conjecture; it is a sop to the gossips. If Thoreau were ever in love with Ellen Sewall, the affair certainly left no perceptible mark on his mature character, and the only reason for keeping so flimsy and unimportant a tradition alive is the romantic notion that somehow it alchemizes Thoreau's asceticism into the nobility of self-sacrifice. At any rate Thoreau never fell in love again. He was often irritated by certain capricious qualities in the feminine temperament, and once he expressed himself bluntly on that point in the Journals. Some years later he was incautious enough to write an essay on sexual love; it is long on idealism and short on experience—in general a silly blunder. Whatever passion he may have had he flamboyantly squandered on Nature.

In fact, there was nothing of the romantic swain about Henry Thoreau for a moment. Ellery Channing describes him in the full vigor of his life as follows: "In height, he was about the average; in his build, spare, with limbs that were rather longer than usual, or of which he made a longer use. His face, once seen, could not be forgotten. The features were quite marked: the nose aquiline or

very Roman, like one of the portraits of Cæsar
(more like a beak, as was said) ; large, over-
hanging brows above the deepest-set blue eyes
that could be seen, in certain lights, and in
others gray—eyes expressive of all kinds of
feeling, but never weak or nearsighted; the
forehead not unusually broad or high, full of
concentrated energy and purpose; the mouth
with prominent lips, pursed up with meaning
and thought when silent, and giving out when
open a stream of the most varied and unusual
and instructive sayings. His hair was a dark
brown, exceedingly abundant, fine, and soft;
and for several years he wore a comely beard.
His whole figure had an active earnestness, as
if he had no moment to waste. The clenched
hand betokened purpose. In walking, he
made a short cut if he could, and when sitting
in the shade or by the wall-side, seemed
merely the clearer to look forward into the
next piece of activity. Even in the boat he
had a wary, transitory air, his eyes on the out-
look—perhaps there might be ducks, or the
Blondin turtle, or an otter, or sparrow."

In the following paragraphs Channing
gives a most concrete account of Thoreau's
strange profession, and the fervor and skill
with which he practiced it: "His habit was to

go abroad a portion of each day, to fields or woods or the Concord River. 'I go out,' he said, 'to see what I have caught in my traps, which I have set for facts.' He looked to fabricate an epitome of creation and give us a homeopathy of Nature. . . . He used the afternoon for walking, and usually set forth about 2.30, returning at 5.30; this three hours was the average length of his walk. In these walks his pockets must accommodate his note-books and spyglass. The notebook was a cover for some folded papers, on which he took his out-of-door notes; this was never omitted, rain or shine. He acquired great skill in convey-ing by a few lines or strokes a long story, which in his written Journal might occupy pages. Into the notebook must go all meas-urements with the foot-rule which he always carried, or the surveyor's tape; also all ob-servations with his spyglass—an invariable companion; all conditions of plants, spring, summer, and fall; the depth of snows, the strangeness of skies—all went down. To his memory he never trusted for a fact, but to the paper and the pencil. I have seen bits of this notebook, but never recognized any word in it; and I have read his expansion in the Jour-nal to many pages of that which occupied him but five minutes to write in the field. 'Have you written up your notes in your Journal?' was one of his questions. . . . He brought home from his walks objects of all kinds— pieces of wood or stone, lichens, seeds, nuts, apples, or whatever he had found; for he was a vigorous collector.

"The idea he conceived was that he might, upon a small territory like Concord, construct a chart or calendar of the phenomena of the seasons in their order, and give their general average for the year. Nothing should be taken on hearsay. How vast a work this is! he could only have completed some portion of it in a long lifetime. His calendar embraced cold and heat, rain and snow, ice and water; he had his gauges on the river, which he consulted winter and summer; he knew the temperature of all the springs in town; he measured the snows when remarkable. I never heard him complain that the plants were too many, the hours too long. . . . Insects were fascinating from the first gray little moth, the Perla, born in February's deceitful glare, to the last luxu-riating Vanessa Antiope, that gorgeous pur-ple-velvet butterfly of November. Hornets, wasps, bees, and spiders, and their several nests he carefully attended. Hawks, ducks, sparrows, thrushes, and migrating warblers, in all their variety, he carefully perused with his field-glass. He 'named all the birds without a gun'—a weapon he never used in mature years. He neither killed nor imprisoned any animal unless driven by acute needs. He brought home a flying squirrel, to study its mode of flight; but quickly carried it back to the wood. His study (a place in the garret) held its dry miscellany of botanical specimens, its corner of canes, its cases of eggs and lichens, and a weight of Indian arrow-heads and hatchets—besides a store of nuts, of which he was quite as fond as squirrels are."

In the succeeding pages of this volume I shall endeavor to show how vividly he lived.

CHAPTER TWO

SPEAKING A GOOD WORD FOR THE TRUTH

SEVERAL years before he died, Thoreau began
to enjoy the prestige of a prophet. Word had
begun to go cautiously round that he was
neither "skulker" nor shanty-misanthrope, as
he sometimes appeared to be; but rather a
man abundantly alive in all his parts, spiritual
as well as physical, and, accordingly, the instrument of truth. The manner of his death
bore some evidence to these opinions. For
three years his health had been steadily de-
clining towards an inevitable end. Three
months before his death he wrote to an unknown correspondent: "You ask particularly
after my health. I suppose that I have not
many months to live; but, of course, I know
nothing about it. I may add that I am enjoying existence as much as ever, and regret nothing." To an unctuously consoling neighbor
he observed simply: "When I was a very little
boy I learned that I must die. So, of course,

I am not disappointed now." When a pious visitor inquired sweetly: "Henry, have you made your peace with God?" he replied: "We have never quarrelled." To one who talked too confidently of the next world, he said: "My friend, one world at a time." When death did actually come, he was whispering something about "Indians" and "moose," perhaps recalling the work he had not had time to arrange in literary form. Having lived as fully as he knew how, having succeeded, as he proposed, "to live deep and suck out all the marrow of life," and having spoken, as he said, "a good word for the truth," he gave himself to death as willingly as he had given himself to life all his years. Many of the pundits who go over his sentences with the scholarly microscope, labelling and classifying as they progress over the rugged contours of his thought, miss the raciness of his style and find no card in their index system to record the tremendous gusto of his career. "I wished to live deliberately," he wrote in *Walden,* "to front only the essential facts of life, and see if I could not learn what it had to teach, and not, when I came to die, discover that I had not lived." So well had he accomplished that reckless purpose that ten or twelve years later death found him not merely resigned, but assured. "Be it life or death, we crave only reality. If we are really dying, let us hear the rattle in our throats and feel cold in the extremities; if we are alive, let us go about our business."

While some were kindled by the lambent flame of beauty in his writing, others were decrying his unsocial eccentricity. For every Emerson and Channing to sing his praises there was a Lowell to thrust out a scornful tongue. And if the full truth were ever to be written of this Concordian (or of any other man as well), some tribute must be paid to both sides of his character, for the one is not more illuminating than the other. In a turgid panegyric published in 1873 Channing dubbed him "Poet-Naturalist," to which others have added "Philosopher." He was none of these things—and all. As a writer his spirit soared "on the viewless wings of Poesy," though he wrote scarcely a verse worth offering at the shrine of poets. Consider the gaunt, homely measures of his poetry, which actually repel the beauty of his thought. Indeed, his prose gave spur to his poetical fancies with more translucence than his verse. As a naturalist his inadequate learning left many holes in his equipment and led him into blunders that now give the small fry of his literary descendants huge bumpers of perverse cheer. As a philosopher he stepped on the toes of his own wisdom now and then, and stubbornly closed his eyes to pertinent evidence on every side. He was, in addition, austere, vituperative, provincial, misanthropic, shrewd, caustic, didactic, suspicious, ill-balanced, idealistic, expectant, eager, full of compassion, tender, patient, serene, and reverent. What a man! Surveyor, carpenter, mason, farmer, school-teacher, manufacturer, lecturer, writer, and dreamer—a whole catalogue of vocations, and how inadequate withal! No wonder he repelled many, irritated some, disturbed others, and drew the sweetness of love from few. We have no sooner focused quietly upon one aspect of his genius than we are bewildered by a myriad of others no less resplendent in their color. And in despair we can only conclude that he lived with a relish of life.

Of his Horatian bean-field behind the Walden cabin Thoreau wrote: "Mine was, as it were, the connecting link between the wild and cultivated fields; as some states are civilized and others half-civilized, and others

savage and barbarous, so my field was, though
not in a bad sense, a half-cultivated field." So
was he, "though not in a bad sense," a half-
cultivated man. If he has any social significance today, three-quarters of a century after
his death, I think it lies in this half-cultivated
sense of one who was divorced from the social
in spite of book-learned wisdom. In this
sense he serves as a standard of comparison,
foster-child of Nature, against whom we may
measure our progress in civilization away
from the principles of our origin. And the
further we drift in our tightly organized manner of living, thrusting the soil further and
further from ourselves, the more Thoreau
emerges alone from the throng of humanity as
the man who longed, not for identity with society, but for union with Nature, for this ever-
healing freedom and release. Let us not tam-
per with the pragmatic value of that cast of
mind, transcendentalism or pantheism according to your choice; and let us not raise the
sweat of argumentation over its ethical value.
Thank God we are not here concerned with
right or wrong! Let us rather acknowledge
the rare success of Thoreau's journey away
from the glitter of society towards the ruddy
glow of nature.

Our shelves sag with countless volumes on
nature by sincere observers in many veins—
White, Thomson, Rousseau, Jeffries, Muir,
Burroughs, Fabre, Hudson—how m a n y
more? I have read many of them with the
keenest delight. Although Hudson comes
closest to the point of alchemization and several times indicates that he understands that
state by intellectual processes, I know no one
but Thoreau who has communicated the essence of nature purely, who, indeed, was so
much a part of nature that he expressed himself best when he was writing of the out-of-
doors. For one brief hour, he tells us in
Walden: "I doubted if the near neighborhood
of man was not essential to a serene and
healthy life." Even as he doubted, however,
Nature was filling his entire consciousness
with her inarticulate vitality: "In the midst
of a gentle rain while these thoughts prevailed, I was suddenly sensible of such a sweet
and beneficent society in Nature, in the very
pattering of the drops, and in every sight and
sound around my house, an infinite and unaccountable friendliness all at once like an at-
mosphere sustaining me, as made the fancied
advantages of human neighborhood insignifi-
cant, and I have never thought of them since."

Vain boasting this may seem to some, and pure
illusion to others. But the limpidness of
Thoreau's style, when he was writing of nature, leads me to believe that he was merely
confessing the truth.

How came he to have this divine genius for
reproducing nature in the sterile words of human language? For, pungent though his style
may be, he could never have written so magic-
ally unless his senses of perception were
extraordinarily acute. And they were, as a
quantity of evidence reveals. As a natural
man, fully developed in all the capacities, he
could walk, skate, row, chop, build a boat,
raise a house, plaster a chimney, repair a
fence, and perform countless other manual
labors with the pride in workmanship characteristic of the skilled artisan. In the woods
and on the mountain he had the physical courage of the man certain of his strength and
skill. It is more to the point of this inquiry,
however, that all his senses were developed to
a high degree: that his sight and touch both
served him well, that his sense of smell, now
comparatively dormant in human beings, was
uncommonly alert, and that, in particular, his
hearing was so sensitive and keen that sweet
sounds transported this gaunt fellow into

ecstasy. All these are familiar qualities,
merely heightened in Thoreau by his persistence in playing upon them and keeping them
unpolluted by social vices. We have no better
testimony of his understanding—of what we
mawkishly term his "sympathy with Nature"
—than Emerson's remark: "Snakes coiled
round his leg; fishes swam into his hand and
he took them out of the water; he pulled the
woodchuck out of its hole by the tail, and
took foxes under his protection from the
hunters."

In the pages of *Walden* and *A Week,* in
the Journals, and occasionally in other Thoreau volumes, I find, not reflections of nature in
the formal, half-sentimental fashion familiar
to readers, but the essence of nature, the whole
gamut of sights, movements, odors, sounds,
and the all-pervading mystery. Literature
has not another line to approach these passages and cannot have until another shall take
the holy orders, as Thoreau took them, and
consecrate himself to the discipline and the
rigid devotions of that service. All the vividness of the out-of-doors is there in the exact
proportion—the smell of beech leaves, the
mutable color of pond water, the gentle hum
of summer, and many qualities of nature that

I, too, have seen, but never brilliantly enough
to form into my own thoughts. Without a
magniloquent phrase to blind the eyes with
rhetoric, he communicates what we lazily call
the "secrets" of nature because we have not
the will to see and have not the patience, as
he had, to follow the year through day by day
as a continuous pageant of changes. Having
distilled his observation of the sumach, for
example, that flourished near his cabin, one
paragraph reports the complete cycle, from
bud to "the large masses of berries, which,
when in flower, had attracted many wild bees,
gradually assuming their bright crimson hue."
And far from giving us disconnected information, like the scientist, he portrays the complete landscape with its proportions and tonal
values, the details and the related phenomena,
washed ever so lightly with Nature's mood.

Sometimes from a hilltop on a summer's
day you may have dreamily noted all the details, the trees, the rocks, and the clumps of
bushes; and then suddenly you may have been
disturbed to find that one of your rocks has
moved a little and has become a man. So well
may a man blend with nature when the season
sits heavily upon him. In that sense Thoreau
occasionally melted into the landscape, grate-

fully losing himself so that he might find himself more certainly; and that is why in Thoreau's works the author does not intrude upon the natural world. "Sometimes in a summer morning, having taken my accustomed bath," he wrote, "I sat in my sunny doorway from sunrise till noon, rapt in a reverie, amidst the pines and hickories and sumachs, in undisturbed solitude and stillness while the birds sang around or flitted noiseless through the house, until by the sun falling in at my west window, or the noise of some traveller's wagon on the distant highway, I was reminded of the lapse of time. I grew in those seasons like corn in the night, and they were far better than any work of the hands would have been. They were not time subtracted from my life, but so much over and above my usual allowance." Was ever a monk more sedulous in his orisons than this novice in Nature's orders? Did ever a penitent give himself more completely to his devotions? But it was a renunciation of worldly life by no means unrewarded. Later on that page Thoreau writes with obvious satisfaction: "If the birds and flowers had tried me by their standard, I should not have been found wanting." To be as pure and wise as a bird or a flower! This

may not be the rosy summit of your dreams.
But Thoreau saw nothing more sublime, and
he succeeded in scaling those heights.

If, as readers, we find ourselves quite transported by the fullness of nature in Thoreau's
style, and in a measure are exhilarated by the
same aspects that kept him tingling with life
to the finger-tips, we must concede that he
drew a satisfaction in which we cannot share.
He was conscious of having a time and a place
in the universe. He was the center of the cos-
mos. He was not merely part of the oversoul,
but the complete oversoul, as we all are, or
shall be. Whether his life was more holy or
not, it at least gave him visually a place in the
scheme of things; and when he returned to the
pandemonium of village life after the Walden
pilgrimage, he did not relinquish his point of
vantage. More and more our social life,
bound round with telegraph wires and rail-
roads, reduces us to units in a vast organization; and although I believe we are never
really humiliated as men, we have scant space
in which to luxuriate. Indeed, the regimenta-
tion of our daily existence begins actually to
put a premium upon liberation by death. In
Thoreau, however, we have a man enjoying

the essence of life rather than its bastard social manifestations; and he knew that he, too, no less than the bean-field, was alive. Even when he was hoeing that Olympian bean-patch, turning the weeds to one side while the black-berries were ripening at the end of the rows, the universe was still in motion. The night-hawk circled overhead; a pair of hen hawks soared through the heavens; wild pigeons passed through the woods; or his hoe turned up a salamander. And when he uncovered an Indian arrow-head or an Indian fire-black-ened stone, he knew that he had a place in history and was merely recultivating old land. So the heavens and the earth conspired to fix his place in eternity, and to honor his pride as a man.

Like a child who sees life simply and whose sensibilities have not become jaded by ex-cesses, he found life a constant adventure, still fairly distant from the North Pole. Does not the child expand his morning's game into a glamorous career? Does he not extract his satisfaction from naïve exaggeration? A scholar, profound in his thinking, Thoreau played at his pastimes no less frankly. Con-sider the whimsical images of *A Week on the Concord and Merrimac Rivers!* What hair-

raising adventures kept that little boating expedition so much on edge in local waters that
Thoreau could, only by cramming, keep its
record within one volume? Two brothers in
their twenties in a homemade craft, with provisions, tent, and sailcloth, pull earnestly
north in fairly placid waters for several days
and then race the autumn homeward. Yet,
like the bold navigators of old, they double
capes, bear to port and starboard, skirt sand-
bars, run before the wind, and bring home
news of foreign men whose accent is not Concordian and who live by strange enterprises in
distant lands. Such a full report, in fact, so
crowded with cosmic connotations, so spiced
with tart poetry, so full of sound, that Thoreau
had no room to set down his intermediary
journey to the White Mountains while his
gallant craft was bobbing up and down in the
Merrimac awaiting the return of her crew.
For a naturalist, one might think, that expedition into the mountains would yield untold
harvest. But he gives us scarcely three pages.
If the proportions had been maintained, such
a work would have burst three volumes and
pied the printer's galley in its eagerness to
get printed. Three brief trips in the Maine
woods fill a volume; three brief excursions to

Cape Cod make another; one cut-rate excursion to Canada discovers a new and fabulous phenomenon at every mile.

Well, we can simply marvel that two years and two months at Walden Pond, with all its discoveries and philosophical reverberations, kept within five hundred printed pages; for the concluding sentence, "The sun is but a morning star," foretells the making of many more books than the Preacher ever dreamed of. *Walden* is merely a preface! Still in his twenties, Thoreau enjoyed this adventure as every small boy believes he would if he had the chance. Do not permit the thunder of Thoreau's eccentric economy to silence the still small voice of his day-by-day enthusiasm. From the March day when he first began to "cut down some tall arrowy white pines, still in their youth, for timber," to the early autumn day when he became again a sojourner in civilized life, he enjoyed his pioneer labors over the ax, tested the satisfaction of building a house with his own hands and feeling every joint, and he revelled in cooking over an open fire, trying the different woods for kindling, setting the rude furniture under the trees and scrubbing the floor with white sand, boating, skating, swimming, and fishing in the pond at his door; and when rain swept over the woods, or snow came whistling down on the north wind and howled at his fieldstone chimney, he knew the luxuries of being warm and cosy in his cabin and hearing the rude elements play boisterously on his roof. How he smacks his lips over the most inconsequential details! "I hewed the main timbers six inches square, most of the studs on two sides only, and the rafters and floor timbers on one side, leaving the rest of the bark on, so that they were just as straight and much stronger than sawed ones. Each stick was carefully mortised or tenoned by its stump, for I had borrowed other tools by this time." Every boy has dreamed of such an adventure, of such a return to the hardy life of our forefathers, and in his twenties Thoreau had not matured too gravely to attempt it. Youth still sent him speeding to youthful enterprises. And if he succeeded in his holiday and rapped his neighbors' knuckles a little for their complete immersion in business, it was because he had had a good time in the Walden woods.

Thoreau did not touch life in many places, as Goethe did, and Sheridan; and unlike them

he dazzled no one with the brilliant versatility
of his genius. Rather did he concentrate upon
the humble tasks that everyone who wished
might perform. Unlike most citizens who
perform these elementary labors, however, he
had the power of understanding, and the facil-
ity for expression. Through him we learn
about them, for the common laborer, even if
he experiences pleasure in his work, is dumb
in the literary language. It would be a mistake, I think, to assume that Thoreau could
have found life sweet only in the way he chose
to follow. He was rather one of the curious
who must find the last secret in everything
they see, who take toys apart to learn the principles of motivation, and who become so skilful that the mechanism of even a hand gre-
nade does not frighten them. It is the virtue
of Thoreau's writings that circumstance and
temperament led him into the one phase of
life that is most elementary in civilization;
and when he had taken that toy apart, he
found the principles of its mechanism likewise elementary and still pertinent to the life
of this day. Such elementary principles, in
fact, so obvious and simple, that they assault
our eardrums like the glycerin bombs of
anarchy. If he had not enjoyed this mode of

living, and had not found it perfectly har-
monious with his temperament, we might dismiss him with the militant gestures of Lowell
and Stevenson. But Thoreau's life had
brought him so much understanding that
when he came to die, his gentle remark: "My
friend, one world at a time," epitomized the
reality of his experience.

CHAPTER THREE

"HENRY IS—WITH DIFFICULTY—SWEET"

HAVING imbibed so much of the elixir of nature, and being by temperament somewhat taciturn and reserved, Thoreau had scant sympathy for man in the social meaning of the term. This was his most forbidding trait; and as a matter of fact it was not inevitable to a man so eager for identity with nature. Beside the slow, stately progress of the seasons the petty embroils and stupid futilities of civilized life become futile indeed; and one can scarcely give all his loyalty to the one without lamenting the other. Thoreau proclaimed his loyalty in no unmistakable terms: "I wish to speak a word for Nature," he began his essay on "Walking," "for absolute freedom and wildness, as contrasted with a freedom and culture merely civil—to regard man as an inhabitant, or a part and parcel of Nature, rather than a member of Society." Upon these terms man as we commonly know him—through our-

selves—can look for little hospitality. And
the truth is that, in the abstract sense at least,
Thoreau gave him little, in spite of the tender
intimacy of several friendships.

Let us not be led astray by the divine afflatus
of his frequent essays on friendship. Let us
not blink the fact that his opinions expressed
about social life represent his true philosophical concepts more accurately than does his
intercourse among men, among those who
sought him out and came to him more or less
professedly as pilgrims. For this point of
view we have the authority of his own words
written in the Journals: "I thrive best on solitude. If I have a companion only one day in
the week, unless it were one or two I could
name, I find that the value of the week to me
has been seriously affected. It dissipates my
days, and often it takes me another week to get
over it. As the Esquimaux of Smith's Strait
in North Greenland laughed when Kane
warned them of their utter extermination, cut
off as they were by ice on all sides from the
race, unless they attempted in season to cross
the glacier southward, so do I laugh when you
tell me of the danger of impoverishing myself
by isolation. It is here that the walrus and
the seal, and the white bear, and the eider

ducks and auks on which I batten, most abound."

I do not wish to fall into the error of condemning a man for an isolated statement. But this entry in the Journals varies a theme common in Thoreau's works; I believe it to be typical of his opinion, if not of his practice. It is, moreover, the sentiment of a self-contained, unsocial being, a troglodyte of sorts; and taken in conjunction with the chilly condemnation of social government in "Civil Disobedience," and the ex-cathedra, snake-in-the-grass vituperation of "Life Without Principle," I think it portrays accurately enough the intellectual Thoreau. In the abstract sense he wished to free himself for communion with himself by washing his hands of man in the mass. "You think I am impoverishing myself by withdrawing from men, but in my solitude I have woven for myself a silken web or chrysalis, and nymph-like shall erelong burst forth a more perfect creature, fitter for a higher society." Men were not sympathetic towards him. He wished to justify himself in his own eyes (and possibly in theirs) by exposing the vanity of their various pretenses.

In a general way he did so. When he attacked society, not in the particular, but in the abstract sense, he smote close to the sources of human unhappiness. "Our life is frittered away by detail," he observed in *Walden*. "An honest man has hardly need to count more than his ten fingers, or in extreme cases he may add his ten toes, and lump the rest. Simplicity, simplicity, simplicity! I say, let your affairs be as two or three, and not a hundred or a thousand; instead of a million count half a dozen, and keep your accounts on your thumb nail. In the midst of this chopping sea of civilized life, such are the clouds and storms and quicksands and thousand-and-one items to be allowed for, that a man has to live, if he would not founder and go to the bottom and not make his port at all, by dead reckoning, and he must be a great calculator indeed who succeeds. Simplify, simplify. . . . The nation itself, with all its so-called internal improvements, which, by the way, are all external and superficial, is just such an unwieldy and overgrown establishment, cluttered with furniture and tripped up by its own traps, ruined by luxury and heedless expense, by want of calculation and a worthy aim, as the million households in the land; and the only cure for it as for them is in a rigid economy, a

stern and more Spartan simplicity of life and
elevation of purpose." Who among us today,
living the rapid and shallow pace of regulated
life, does not echo every one of these words
and agree that the sources of social unhappiness are accurately stated in this passage?
Every arm-chair philosopher, amiable and
lazy, knows all this to be true in his heart.
And when Thoreau addressed his compatriots
thus wisely from the oracle of Nature, some
of the sweetness and pity of that all-forgiving
goddess informs his style. Indeed, the lucid
thinking and the compassion of some of those
passages affect me deeply whenever I read
them; then I am not irritated by the cold at-
titudinizing that proves so forbidding in his
lucubrations, or when he tries to speak tartly
from the rostrum; when, in sum, he is preach-
ing with no more knowledge of his parish-
ioners' woes than the average intellectual
divine.

For the hostility and the jeering of "Civil
Disobedience," "Life Without Principle,"
and "Slavery in Massachusetts" betoken
nothing more admirable than want of sympathy, and arid understanding. Was not
Thoreau a little pious in these papers? Was
he not setting himself up? Was he not pusil-

lanimous, vindictive, and feline in his attack? Alas! most of his public appearances (by which his neighbors knew him) were unworthy of the poet who sang of Nature in *Walden* and recorded the mysteries of the Concord and Merrimac Rivers in chryselephantine style. Only a man of limited experience, astringent in his living, could have written: "The ways by which you may get money almost without exception lead downward." There is spleen in: "The rush to California, for instance, not merely of merchants, but of philosophers and prophets, so-called, in relation to it, reflects the greatest disgrace on mankind"; "The government does not concern me much, and I shall bestow the fewest possible thoughts on it." In such passages we miss the give-and-take, the *camaraderie* of men all headed hopefully in the same direction, that informs the writings of men who know more of their neighbors. "Come, come, Henry!" I feel like saying, "if Nature countenances these little failings and forgives all with her sweet beneficence, how much more then ought you, the disciple of Nature, to yield and try to understand as well. This is no time for puffing and preening." In social conversation Thoreau's pugnacity, censoriousness, and propensity for paradoxical statement all made the easy unburdening of thought a vexatious task. Said Emerson: "Henry is—with difficulty—sweet." All this acidity renders equally difficult his public animadversions on society. No wonder he was put down as a crank and boor by many of his townsfolk.

To limit our consideration of Thoreau's relations with men to this quite unflattering, though most conspicuous, attitude would be to miss the best part of his spiritual character. More significant than his intellectual statements are the facts of his career. He may have had something of the sort in mind when he wrote in his Journals: "The real facts of a poet's life would be of more value to us than any work of his art. I mean that the very scheme and form of his poetry, so-called, is adopted at a sacrifice of vital truth and poetry. Shakespeare has left us his fancies and imaginings, but the truth of his life, with its becoming circumstances, we know nothing about. The writer is reported, the liver not at all." Nearly all of Thoreau's political thoughts reveal the less worthy side of his character. Sometimes I fancy that the belated cultivation of his society by credulous readers attracted to his dogma made him increasingly self-conscious—in fact forced him psychologically to take sides, like a self-ordained prophet, between man and Nature. At any rate, his public appearances were generally inferior to his life. It is more illuminating of Thoreau's private character to remember that he gave generously of himself, that he paid his neighbors in the only specie his mint delivered, in manual labor and tinkering, or as Edward Emerson reports: "He overpaid his keep in mere handiwork, which he convinced all friends that it was a favor to him to allow him to do for them (such as burning out chimneys, setting stoves, door-knobs, or shutters to right), to make no mention of higher service."

In private life Thoreau was as tender as a poet, as loving of his friends, as appreciative of their virtue; and his relations with his family bespeak a man of highest character and sensibilities. "Ah, my friends, I know you better than you think, and love you better, too. The day after never we shall have an explanation." Those who picture him as a stoic, a gaunt figure silhouetted against the skyline, reckon without the volume of his collected letters, the testimony of Channing and other friends, and the more cordial facts of his relationships. Although he was seldom demonstrative (everyone was aghast when he danced a jig once at a party) his letters especially tremble with a sincerity of emotion rare among man, and a patience and desire to be helpful that is positively disarming. The world is better that such a man should have lived and made a few enduring friendships. Since the first half of the nineteenth century I think we have lost one of the most priceless qualities of human nature—the sweetness of family life, a personal and social entity far-reaching in its effect upon the national character. In Thoreau we find filial love and responsibility deeply ingrained; for his letters to his parents, sisters, and brother express a strong desire to be helpful and they also breathe the delicate aroma of tender affection. To Helen and Sophia reluctantly away from home he wrote the details of Concord and domestic phenomena, dear to both of them— the height of the snow measured against the fence-post or the flowering of Concord plants. The few letters he wrote to his brother John (companion on river and in field), convey an emotion and an enthusiasm that come as a surprise to those familiar only with the more mature Thoreau. What a fine relationship this must have been! It will be remembered that John Thoreau died a painful death from lock-jaw three years after the boating excursion on the Concord and Merrimac Rivers. To understand the poignancy of Henry's grief, and the pain that lingered all the rest of his life, one has only to read the exuberant boyish letters written to John in 1838, letters that fairly transfigure the common noun "brother." No one can say how much store Henry set by his brother, how much pure affection passed between them; and no one can quite estimate the effect John's death had upon Henry's entire career. Sometimes when I read the more frigid thoughts of Thoreau's later life I find myself wishing that John might have lived to help this brooding youth through the village streets. Then there might have been a warmer glow in the social thoughts of Henry Thoreau.

Most of his friendships, which he valued, nourished, and thus rendered sacred, flourished upon his own terms. Excepting Emerson, his friends largely subordinated themselves to his temperament, gave what they could, took what they might, and frequently made shift with much they did not understand. Despite Thoreau's mellifluous literary tribute to friendship, far more emotional and gracious, I think, than Emerson's, he was unwittingly an imperious master. For example, between Channing and Thoreau the bond of friendship was well-nigh indissoluble; no one else enjoyed so much intimacy with Henry abroad and few others would he introduce to the private riches of the countryside. Together they went to Canada, Cape Cod, the White Mountains, and Monadnock, and in the fields and on the rivers about Concord, close and forebearing comrades, mutually appreciative. When Thoreau writes of him, certain familiar, endearing expressions turn up that are not common in this shy man's vocabulary. "He and I, as you know, have been old cronies"; "the Channing you have seen and described is the real Simon Pure"; "nor need I suggest how worthy and poetic he is, and what an inexhaustible fund of good fellowship you will find in him." And yet even the loyal Channing confesses to a certain hardness in Thoreau's character apparent in the field on those occasions when sympathy is often indispensable: "In his later journeys, if his companion was footsore or loitered, he steadfastly pursued his road. Once when a follower [obviously Channing] was done up with a headache and incapable of motion, hoping his associate would comfort him and perhaps afford him a sip of tea, he said: 'There are people who are sick in that way every morning, and go about their affairs,' and then marched off about his. In such limits, so inevitable, was he compacted." One can understand this petty trait of character without excusing it; are not the strong contemptuous of the weak? Since Thoreau laid so much stress upon his excursions, found in them the treasures he regarded as most holy, any human ills that retarded his progress must have vexed him more than we know. Such cavalier treatment, however, is unworthy of one who wept at the parting of a friendship, and cherished the precious ties of spiritual communication as immortal bonds of divinity. Indeed, upon so high a plane did he place such unions that when one of his dearest friendships had come to an end (although, as a matter of fact, it was later resumed) he regarded even this as a sign from the immortal gods, mysterious, holy, and final: "I do not know what has made my friend doubt me, but I know that in love there is no mistake, and that every estrangement is well founded. But my destiny is not narrowed; rather, if possible, the broader for it. The heavens withdraw and arch themselves higher. I am sensible not only of a moral, but even of a grand physical pain, such as gods may feel, about my head and breast, a certain ache and fullness. This rending of a tie, it is not my work, nor thine. It is no accident that we mind; it is only the awards of fate that are affecting. I know of no æons or periods, no life or death, but these meetings and separations." "It is the merit and preservation of Friendship," he said upon another occasion, "that it takes place on a level higher than the actual characters of the parties would seem to warrant." Of such purity and spiritual ambition were Thoreau's mystic fancies.

Some pages before we said we should not be led astray by the vaulting style of his philosophy. Here we are to consider the facts of his relationships. I think his friendship with Emerson reveals him most completely. Thoreau was not quite great enough to stand that test. Always a truth-teller, benign, confident, and appreciative, Emerson several times records the rough edgings in his dealings with Thoreau; the association was no suave meeting of gentlemen. But in his early years Thoreau was at his best in Emerson's company, reflecting the celestial greatness of this neighbor, obedient to his own principles, never storming the citadel as he did against weaker armies, and manifesting his love in the thoughtful ways common between men on intimate terms. When Thoreau writes to Emerson from Staten Island, his salutation, "My dear Friend," echoes the deepest harmony or the richest melody possible in those casual words.

Which was the greater man? As long as the works of the two are printed and the memory of their Concord career lingers, that will be the moot point; it will reveal, I fancy, the sympathies of the contestants rather than the ultimate truth of these philosophers. For although Thoreau and Emerson travelled the same road, exchanging their intellectual baggage freely and straining their eyes for the same holy city, the truth seems to be that they were two *men*, citizens in their own right, one broad and tranquil, the other deep and passionate. One phase of their similarity and distinction can be no more accurately expressed than in Emerson's own journal: "In reading Henry Thoreau's journal, I am very sensible of the vigor of his constitution. That oaken strength which I noted whenever he

walked, or worked, or surveyed wood-lots, the
same unhesitating hand with which a field-
laborer accosts a piece of work which I should
shun as a waste of strength, Henry shows in
his literary task. He has muscle, and ven-
tures and performs feats which I am forced
to decline. In reading him I find the same
thoughts, the same spirit, that is in me, but
he takes a step beyond and illustrates by ex-
cellent images that which I should have conveyed in a sleepy generalization. 'Tis as if I
went into a gymnasium, and saw youths leap
and climb and swing with a force unapproach-
able, though their feats are only a continua-
tion of my initial grapplings and jumps."
Similarly of their lives: Emerson surveyed a
broad landscape, was more patient, sympathetic, radiant, indeed; and accordingly he
contemplated life through the eyes of his fellows as well as his own. On the other hand,
Thoreau plowed one furrow deeply and deliberately, studying passionately what lay at
his feet and drawing the moral cleanly from
the limited evidence at his disposal. Hot
words have passed between the modern cham-
pions on both sides, the contenders each claim-
ing for his own idol the ultimate canonization.
It is charged that Thoreau imitated Emerson,

acquired similar tricks of voice and manner, so that the neighbors snickered up their sleeves; and "it would have been strange," writes Emerson's son, "if the village youth should not have been influenced by the older thinker for a time. . . . But Thoreau was incapable of conscious imitation. His faults, if any, lay in exactly the opposite direction. Both men were fearless thinkers, at war indeed against many of the same usages, and interested in the emancipation of the individual. Both went to great Nature to be refreshed and inspired." Neither gave in to the world. Since Emerson and Thoreau lived side by side, for the most part harmoniously, and loved each other deeply withal, it behooves us lesser disciples to make good that same wisdom by keeping Thoreau and Emerson even now on a non-competitive basis.

Although as citizens of Concord they had known each other for some years before their first true meeting occurred, they did not become acquainted intellectually until 1837. After Emerson had delivered a new lecture in Concord, Helen Thoreau remarked to a close friend of Mrs. Emerson: "There is a thought almost identical with that in Henry's Journal." (Henry was the younger by fourteen

years.) Always alert to goodness of character Emerson read his neighbor's Journal with
quick appreciation. Do not mistake the quality of their friendship. At least among men,
there was no touch-and-go about Thoreau.
But the intimacy flourished; in 1838 Emerson
reported: "I delight much in my young
friend, who seems to have as free and erect a
mind as any I have ever met." For several
years Thoreau's life matured in close proxim-
ity to Emerson. They exchanged thoughts, if
not compliments, with mutual confidence and
understanding. While Emerson was abroad,
Thoreau lived in the Emerson house, keeping
the establishment in order and reporting to
his friend across the water those flavorsome
domestic details calculated to console and re-
assure a father. I am struck in those letters
with Thoreau's judgment in the items he reported, for especially when he conveys news
of the children he speaks directly to the heart
of a parent. Of little "Eddy": " 'If Waldo
were here,' said he the other night at bedtime,
'we'd be four going upstairs.' Would he like
to tell papa anything? No, not anything; but
finally, yes, he would—that one of the white
horses in his new barouche is broken!" That
is vital information, coolly judged and neatly

reported in Thoreau's usual style. Perhaps
the next is less well calculated to console a
father's mind : of Eddy again—"He very seriously asked me the other day : 'Mr. Thoreau,
will you be my father?' I am occasionally
Mr. Rough-and-tumble with him that I may
not miss *him,* and lest he should miss *you* too
much. So you must come back soon, or you
will be superseded." Mrs. Emerson, like her
good friend Mrs. Lucy Brown, was always
fond of Henry and perhaps less consciously
but more profoundly than her husband.
When Henry was still in pain after the agony
of his brother's death, Mrs. Emerson knew
best how to comfort him. Later they exchanged, if not nobler thoughts, at least ten-
derer sentiments than came from Emerson.
From Staten Island Thoreau writes to her in
an evanescent mood : "I could hardly believe,
after the lapse of one night, that I had such a
noble letter still at hand to read—that it was
not some fine dream. I looked at midnight
to be sure that it was real. . . . My friend, I
have read your letter as if I was not reading
it. After each pause I could defer the rest
forever. The thought of you will be a new
motive for each right action. You are another
human being whom I know, and might not

our topic be as broad as the universe?" Thus with the Emersons he had the freedom of mind and spirit by which his poetry flowered in its freshest hour.

Although Thoreau's relations with Channing, Harrison Blake, and Daniel Ricketson discover good qualities in his temperament, this Emerson brotherhood, putting Thoreau to the test, is the most revealing. Perhaps because of all his friends Emerson yielded less to Thoreau's moods and pugnacity, separated the wheat from the chaff and took both at their true value. Thoreau unconsciously patronized when he could. In the long and cordial letters to Blake and Ricketson, seething with emotion and straining towards moral purity, perhaps you will catch the overtones of smugness in which the generosity in thought does not sufficiently impoverish the giver. With Emerson, however, his peer in moral philosophy and his superior in social wisdom, Thoreau could scarcely assume the sacrosanct manner. In those letters from Staten Island in 1843 all the trouble, hope, and faith of the young man exude from every paragraph—health, finance, reports of progress, self-analysis; and the opinions expressed lose none of their strength but all their dogmatism in this

free exchange with a great mind—opinions on
men, literature, nature, New York, sometimes
verging on plain gossip. Yes, here Thoreau
was at his best, in contact with one who found
only the best in the men he knew. Always
protecting himself against humiliation, proud
and timid, Thoreau poured out his substance
freely where he knew it to be welcome. The
mutual satisfaction in this early friendship
may be indicated by a thousand sentences from
Emerson's pen, in his sublime memorial paper
definitely; but more informally in one simple
letter written home from England: "Dear
Henry,—Very welcome in the parcel was
your letter, very precious your thoughts and
tidings. It is one of the best things connected
with my coming hither that you could and
would keep the homestead; that fireplace
shines all the brighter, and has a certain permanent glimmer therefor. Thanks, ever
more thanks for the kindness which I well dis-
cern to the youth of the house: to my darling
little horseman of pewter, wooden, rocking,
and what other breeds—destined, I hope, to
ride Pegasus yet, and, I hope, not destined to
be thrown: to Edith, who long ago drew from
you verses which I carefully preserve: to
Ellen, whom by speech, and now by letter, I

find old enough to be companionable, and to choose and reward her own friends in her own fashions. She sends me a poem today, which I have read three times!"

In spite of this cordial glow of comradeship on the highest terms, I suspect Thoreau at last proved unworthy of the supreme intimacy. By 1855 Emerson and Thoreau were spasmodically estranged; and, although the information is meager, I am inclined to put the blame on Thoreau's censorious nature. In his guarded chronicles in the Journals he complains of petty slights, of patronizing airs; and, more specifically, he says that Emerson received visits but never made them, and that he made gifts but refused to accept others in return. Such complaints are trifling by comparison with Thoreau's repeated decisions to conclude the friendship; obviously his vanity had been wounded. However, we must remember that by this time Emerson's fame had spread throughout America and to parts of Europe; that he was sought as a lecturer by audiences even beyond the Mississippi; and received hospitably in England and France. In fine, Emerson smacked a bit of the gentleman, and had acquired some of the graces that

Thoreau instinctively distrusted—"within such limits," as Channing declared, "was he compacted." Emerson, for his part, was a little weary of Thoreau's pugnacity. In 1856 he expressed his displeasure in this entry in the Journal: "If I knew only Thoreau, I should think co-operation of good men impossible. Must we always talk for victory, and never once for truth, for comfort and joy? Centrality he has, and penetration, strong understanding and the higher gifts—the insight of the real, or from the real, and the moral rectitude that belongs to it; but all this and all his resources of wit and invention are lost to me, in every experiment, year after year, that I make, to hold intercourse with his mind. Always some weary captious paradox to fight you with, and the time and temper wasted." So far had their friendship travelled since the enthusiasm of its early years. There is no full record of its difficulties; the immediate causes are vague and cloudy. But to me there seems to have been no sufficient reason for distrusting such an open neighbor as Emerson. In view of their first intimacy, I suspect Thoreau of having reached too soon the limits of his faith in a great man; and as an admirer of Thoreau I am disappointed.

However much Thoreau's social relations may result in revising our conception of him as a man, we must nevertheless admire his quick judgment of human character. Indeed, that ability reflects the greatest credit upon him, and verifies his genius as a natural philosopher. Despite the truculence of his social objurgations, this instinctive understanding of human nature, this ability to perceive the true at a glance, this uncanny precision, proves him, I think, to have been genuine in his thinking. Conceding to him the privilege of practicing his own principles and setting up his own standards of social virtue, I know of no instance in which he underestimated man or woman. "At first glance," Emerson said, "he measured his companion, and, though insensible to some fine traits of culture, could very well report his weight and calibre. . . . He understood the matter at a glance, and saw the limitations and poverty of those he talked with, so that nothing seemed concealed from such terrible eyes." He could rebuke patronage and artificiality without uttering a word of censure. Likewise he understood the genuine instantly, and could discriminate between what was good and what unworthy. For example, nothing is more reassuring than his recognition of Walt Whitman's immensity as the result of one fleeting visit to Brooklyn, although, as he said: "I did not get far in conversation with him—two more being present." Notwithstanding the mutual embarrassment of this visit, Thoreau came very near to summing up Walt's personality and character: "He is apparently the greatest democrat the world has ever seen. Kings and aristocracy go by the board at once, as they have long deserved to. A remarkably strong, though coarse, nature, of a sweet disposition, and much prized by his friends. Though peculiar and rough in his exterior, his skin (all over (?)) red, he is essentially a gentleman. I am still somewhat in a quandary about him—feel that he is essentially strange to me, at any rate; but I am surprised by the sight of him. He is very broad, but, as I have said, not fine." Thus in 1856, while the literary and social world was still resenting Whitman, Thoreau anticipated the judgment of posterity, in both the great and common qualities.

Such people, still closely related to Nature, seemed the most real to Thoreau; he could describe them with the same objectivity and pellucidity that distinguished his genius for natural reporting. I am amazed by the adroit skill with which he selected the essential details of their characters. He did not go astray on the nobility of John Brown; while others hesitated he spoke fearlessly for this simple-minded idealistic martyr. What completer re-creation of a man can we discover in literature than his *Walden* portrait of the Canadian woodchopper? Remember the scholarly lock-tender in *A Week* whom Thoreau encountered in passing; I think he set off the *man* in that figure as completely as though the meeting were a long one. One night's lodging at Wellfleet yields a complete transference on paper of an old oysterman, his knowledge, ignorance, garrulousness, domestic relations; and a brilliant summary of his character. All the old fishermen, woodchoppers, hunters, and social derelicts about Concord turn up in sympathetic studies in the Journal. Since Thoreau studied character from the most searching viewpoint, he was interested in men in the raw, men who still proclaimed in their lives allegiance to Nature; and he etched them with economical, deep-bitten strokes. He caught them on the wing with accurate shots. But never more surely than in the study of Joe Polis, the Indian guide who carried Thoreau

and Edward Hoar over the Allegash and East
Branch in 1857. Although Thoreau was always interested in Indians, he never came in
closer contact with unsullied Indian character
than on the trip with Polis, "who was one of
the aristocracy." "I told him that in this voyage," writes Thoreau, "I would tell him all
I knew, and he should tell me all he knew, to
which he readily agreed." And so this flavorsome account of the deep woods adventure
becomes likewise an analysis of character and
a study in miniature of the entire Indian civilization, from its language and surface phenomena to its traditions, its superstitions, its
strength and weakness, all unswervingly distinguished and recorded. Stolid and impas-
sive though Polis was, Thoreau recognized
him as a fully developed, natural man. In his
last years, Emerson tells us, Thoreau was im-
pressed by three men—Walt Whitman, John
Brown, and Joe Polis. From what he wrote
about these men we may have confidence in
his judgment and his understanding; and those
who dismiss Thoreau as a stoic may be assured
here of his underlying human sympathy. If
his protestations against society, and his manner of life, seem to betoken the misanthrope,
his descriptions of the men he admired relieve

him from the ugly charge of posing. With
man, as with nature, he was searching. He
required, in his Yankee phrase, "the genuine
article."

CHAPTER FOUR

STRANGE VERSE AND PLAIN PROSE

EARLY in the eighteen-forties Thoreau came
to think of himself as a writer. If one who ex-
celled equally in manual labor and in thinking
from observation (or as pure "receptive consciousness," to use a highly abstract term) may
be put down as a member of any profession, it
is no mistake to call him a writer. Thoreau
was a "writing man" in the idiom of the vil-
lagers. Before he took up his abode at Walden, he was contributing strange verse and
plain prose to the *Dial,* that utopian organ of
the Transcendentalists; and he was winning,
withal, quite as many guffaws as plaudits.
Margaret Fuller, the most practical and the
most brilliant of these cerebralists, could not
stifle a ribald smile or two. But with all the
pugnacious determination of which he was
capable Thoreau was working steadily at his
Journal, recasting his sentences laboriously,
discarding the false ones, expanding and con-

tracting with a view to expressing his thoughts exactly so that he might understand them himself. "Those authors are successful who do not write down to others, but make their own taste and judgment their audience. . . . It is enough if I please myself with writing; I am then sure of an audience." Or again: "Nothing goes by luck in composition; it allows of no trick. The best you can write will be the best you are. Every sentence is the result of long probation. The author's character is read from title-page to end. Of this he never corrects the proofs. We read it as the essential character of handwriting without regard to the flourishes." This was no pose with Thoreau, but the unembellished structure of his thought and convictions. All his books express his thought on the precise terms set down in these two casual entries in the Journal. No writer, I believe, has ever conveyed the essentials of his thought more completely. Each sentence carries a full load. Even his nebulous transcendentalisms mark their swift course with the blaze of a sky rocket. His verse seems to me execrable; his prose is glorious. I enjoy it for its literary beauty, its rippling rhythm, and its firm cargo of meaning.

Thoreau was a writer on his own exacting model.

Like the course of his life, the form of his literary composition belongs within none of the familiar categories. We may catalogue the chief elements—narration, description, speculation, history, science, essay, argumentation, poetry. When the Secretary of the Association for the Advancement of Science asked him for specific information about his professional interests he confessed to his Journal: "The fact is I am a mystic, a transcendentalist, and a natural philosopher to boot." But although he scorned science, because it ignored the "higher law," he pursued the scientific method in all his books, always in the direction of the higher law, always scraping up all the information he could find in the blind hope that it might lead him closer to the eternal mysteries. Sometimes he came perilously near to discovering them.

In addition to *Walden*, published in 1854, his only formal books were *A Week on the Concord and Merrimac Rivers*, published in 1849, and *Cape Cod* and *The Maine Woods*, published posthumously. For the rest we have *Familiar Letters*, the collections entitled *Excursions* and *Miscellanies*, and the un-

wieldy length of the Journals from which several of his books were in large part compiled.
Cape Cod and *The Maine Woods* alone remain sufficiently loyal to their titular theme.
In all the other writings he left the main chan-
nel whenever a pleasant creek lured him to
side adventuring. For the readers who are
not exclusively concerned with the writer's
cast of mind, this discursive, often dogmatic,
method becomes maddening. I shall not soon
forget my dismay upon reading *A Week* for
the first time. Nothing seemed to interest
Thoreau less than the boyish boating-voyage
that interested me most. Only the limpid
transcription of those watery passages repaid
me for the tough lucubrations on history, style,
religion, the Greek poets, and the Bhagavad-
Gita. These literary embellishments did better, I fancied, in the sober pages of the *Dial*
than in the log-book of a brave and rivery adventure. Perhaps others thought so too; for,
as every reader of Thoreau knows, no publisher would risk his money on that bewilder-
ing volume by an unknown author. And four
years after 1,000 copies had been published
at Thoreau's expense, 700 were returned to
him by the publisher as unsalable. As a matter of fact, only 115 copies had been sold for

cash. "I can see now what I write for, and the result of my labors," he declared; "nevertheless, in spite of this result, sitting beside the inert mass of my works, I take up my pen tonight, to record what thought or experience I may have had, with as much satisfaction as ever. Indeed, I believe that the result is more inspiring and better than if a thousand had bought my wares. It affects my privacy less, and leaves me freer." Well, let us not deny him this self-healing gesture. He worked steadily for several years to pay for that literary folly.

In one sense, at least, this first adventure into the literary world may be considered Thoreau's most characteristic book. In all the other works, except the Journals, Thoreau endeavored, however unsuccessfully, to give some form to the free developments of the main theme. Although many pages of *Walden,* for example, wander far, far from the hut by the cove, the entire book enjoys a unity of thought and experience. With the arrogance of youth, however, Thoreau made no pretense in *A Week* of clinging to the main theme. Slender, indeed, are the threads connecting the translations from Anacreon, the excursions in western Massachusetts, the es-

says on history and biography, to the inva-
sion of New Hampshire by boat. During the
ten years between the voyage and the publication of the book Thoreau had well-nigh forgotten the domestic details of his voyage and
had become absorbed in philosophy. How
amusing the connecting links are, how pedan-
tic withal: "While engaged in these reflections . . ."; "While we float here, far from
the tributary stream on whose banks our
friends and kindred dwell, our thoughts, like
the stars, come out of the horizon . . .";
"This noontide was fit occasion to make some
pleasant harbor, and there read the journal of
some voyager like ourselves . . ."; "So we
sailed this afternoon, thinking of the saying of
Pythagoras, . . ." etc. With the exception
of the transfiguring disquisitions on friendship, sensitive in conception and beautiful in
expression, these exercises in literary composition do not concern us now. Nevertheless,
amorphous and perplexing as *A Week* may
be, it stands as an earnest of what Thoreau
was to be. Already his passion for the an-
cients, his distrust of professed religion, his
impatience with social ambitions, his confidence in Nature, and his interest in the homely
details of business and commerce, were com-

ing to the surface. Some of the most highly
charged sentences promise a vigorous, uncom-
promising mind, and reveal his cast of
thought: "There is in my nature, methinks, a
singular yearning towards all wildness";
"Books, not which afford us a cowering enjoyment, but in which each thought is of unusual daring; such as an idle man cannot read,
and a timid one would not be entertained by,
which even make us dangerous to existing in-
stitutions—such call I good books"; "The poet
is he that hath fat enough, like bears and mar-
mots, to suck his claws all winter"; "Men
have a respect for scholarship and learning
greatly out of proportion to the use they commonly serve"; "Where shall we look for
standard English, but to the works of a
standard man"; "Give me a sentence which no
intelligence can understand"; "Even the utmost good-will and harmony and practical
kindness are not sufficient for Friendship, for
Friends do not live in harmony merely, as
some say, but in melody"; "The language of
Friendship is not words but meanings"; "The
unconsciousness of man is the consciousness of
God," etc.

For many of us the diaphanous color of his
descriptive and narrative passages brings

greater joy, for it serves as evidence of his mystic association with Nature, and his genius for interpretation by simple reporting. As a rule he does not moralize in these descriptive passages; they stand complete in themselves. And just as they convey the images of river and bank perfectly, without effort, so do they also vibrate with Thoreau's youthful enthusiasm. Let us pluck one casual passage from the midst of a long narrative: "Thus we held on, sailing or dipping our way along with the paddle in this broad river—smooth and placid, flowing over concealed rocks, where we could see the pickerel lying low in the transparent water—eager to double some distant cape, to make some great bend as in the life of man, and see what the new perspective would open; looking far into a new country, broad and serene, the cottages of settlers seen afar for the first time, yet with the moss of a century on their roofs, and the third or fourth generation in their shadow." Here, within the compass of one sentence, is the child of Nature, the reporter of natural beauties, and the "Great Expector," as he later termed Alcott, all the facets characteristic of *Walden*. Were it not for *Walden, A Week* might not endure. As the *Athenæum* said in its review columns: "The matter is for the most part poor enough, but there are a few things in the volume, scattered here and there, which suggest that the writer is a man with a habit of original thinking." In the thrifty words of the Yankee, that may be considered a "conservative statement"!

For some readers of Thoreau, *Cape Cod* appears to be his most satisfactory book, *Walden* to one side for the moment. Within certain definite limits it seems one of the best to me also; for, by virtue of the theme, it conveys most vibrantly the sense of wonder underlying all Thoreau's works. When he was sailing the Concord and Merrimac Rivers, and when he was penetrating the wilds of northeastern Maine, he was in the midst of country not unlike that of Concord. On those excursions he was dealing in trees, flowers, birds, ponds, and hills; only the proportions and the details differed. At Cape Cod, however, he encountered the seaside, a land dominated by the surging ocean, strange to a landsman, who, as he said, "having come so fresh to the sea, I have got but little salted." Looking back to his tight little world of Concord, he continues, not without pride: "My readers

must expect only so much saltiness as the land
breeze acquires from blowing over an arm of
the sea, or is tasted on the windows and the
bark of trees twenty miles inland, after the
September gales."

Let us reflect for a moment upon the approach to Cape Cod of a man like Thoreau.
For several months he had lived on Staten
Island, a New York suburb, as the tutor to
Judge Emerson's children; otherwise his experience of the sea had been thoroughly
casual, as an arrogantly inland man comes to
observe it. Moreover, the more profoundly
he studied the phenomena of his neighborhood ("With the utmost industry we cannot
expect to know an area more than six miles
square"), the more he came to regard it as a
microcosm. Walden Pond, with its bays,
sand-bars, wave action, and varying surface,
served the function of an ocean. During his
three excursions to Cape Cod, however, total-
ling in all about three weeks, he discovered
the ocean and the shore, with its natives, its
commerce, its natural history, a fresh phenomenon, serving another master entirely—the
ocean. He had not expected that much difference. As *Cape Cod* records his excursions,
his emotions were, at first, amusement and

contempt, patronizing and inquisitive. Why
did these brine-drenched men of the sea build
their houses like New England farm build-
ings? How ridiculous their attempts at agri-
culture! How scrawny and pinched their
woodlands! In the space of three weeks
Thoreau could scarcely readjust his perspective to match theirs exactly; here, at least, was
a landscape in which he did not blend. Under the circumstances his curiosity, which was
the mainspring of his existence, ran rampant
until every moment was spent in observation;
and he humbly apologized to his readers for
not having tasted the water of one brook that
he crossed and for not being able to report, as
a careful writer should, whether it was sweet
or salt. With his usual passion for performing every task thoroughly, if only to satisfy
himself, he went to all the sources on Cape
Cod, publications of the historical society,
agricultural reports, old gazetteers, the chronicles of early explorers; and armed with this
ammunition, some of which at least he carried
himself, he walked through the townships,
knowing more of their history and natural
produce than the natives. One characteristic
incident may indicate the bend of his thought.
On the beach near Wellfleet he cooked and

ate a large clam that later made him ill. "I
was pleased to read afterwards," he records
with glee, "in Mourt's Relation of the landing of the Pilgrims in Provincetown Harbor,
these words: 'We found great muscles' (the
old editor says that they were undoubtedly
sea-clams) 'and very fat and full of sea-pearl;
but we could not eat them, for they made us
all sick that did eat, as well sailors as passen-
gers . . . but they were soon well again.' It
brought me nearer the Pilgrims to be thus reminded by a similar experience that I was so
like them. . . . I was also pleased to find that
man and the clam lay still at the same angle
to one another."

Like the perfect reporter that he could be,
Thoreau gathered all the news of the Cape;
not forgetting a shipwreck at Cohasset that
turned him aside during most of the first
chapter. He described the inhabitants, with
their dominant traits, the customs, the details
of the fisheries, the cut of the surf, the problems of the lighthouse keeper, the action of the
sand, the habits of the clam, the profits of
clamming, the full flavor of the old Wellfleet
oysterman, who was under "petticoat rule,"
the gruesome romance of the wrecks, the
mackerel fleet, oddities such as fill the back

columns of country newspapers, the tides, the
sea—it is all there in plain "homespun prose."
Thoreau, travelling in a foreign clime, one
hundred miles from Concord, sought to bring
home all the really significant details of this
unaccountable landspit so that all might understand it and taste the full savor of its salt.
On the beach near Nauset he began to experience the inner meanings of this region:
"There I had got the Cape under me, as much
as if I were riding it barebacked. It was not
as on the map or seen from the stage-coach;
but there I found it all out of doors, huge and
real, Cape Cod! as it cannot be represented on
a map, color it as you will; the thing itself,
than which there is nothing more like it, no
truer picture or account; which you cannot go
farther and see. I cannot remember what I
thought before that it was. They commonly
celebrate those beaches only which have a
hotel on them, not those which have a humane
house alone. But I wished to see that seashore
where man's works are wrecks; to put up at
the true Atlantic House, where the ocean is
land-lord as well as sea-lord, and comes ashore
without a wharf for a landing; where the
crumbling land is the only invalid, or at best
is but dry land, and that is all you can say of

it." Thus when Thoreau had got through
with the object under observation, having discovered its peculiarities rather than its resemblances, portraying the wreckers, the fishermen, and the husbandmen at full length,
there was some point in his arrogant assump-
tion that no one else had discovered Cape Cod
and that he was the publisher of its contours.
In the last few pages he gives directions and
advice to prospective visitors; for, as he says,
quite correctly, "The time must come when
this coast will be a place of resort for those
New Englanders who really wish to visit the
seaside." The facts of the summer-resort
trade bear out the truth of his prophecy. How
many of the summer visitors, inhabiting Cape
Cod year after year, return with as much of
its spirit as Thoreau sipped off in three weeks?
How many know, as he did, that "A man may
stand there and put all America behind him"?

One night in the woods of Maine Thoreau
beheld "a white and slumberous light, like a
glow-worm's." Immediately he knew that it
must be phosphorescent wood, which he had
heard of frequently, but had never seen. In a
high state of enthusiasm he got out of his
blanket, cut the wood out with his knife, ex-

amined the log, and held the particles in the
hollow of his hand, where they lit it up, revealing the lines and wrinkles brilliantly.
Indeed, so far was he transported by this dis-
covery that he waked up his companion to ex-
hibit them, not doubting for a moment the
universal importance of that bit of forest
magic. (His companion's remarks unfortu-
nately are not recorded.)

Although that incident brought Thoreau
perhaps more ecstasy than anything else he
saw, I think it is characteristic of the pleasure
he enjoyed during his journeys into the Maine
woods, quite adequately recorded in the volume bearing that title. During the Walden
sojourn he made an excursion of two weeks to
Mt. Ktaadn, anticipating, as with Cape Cod,
the modern course of summer traffic. In 1853
he made a canoe journey with a moose-hunt-
ing Indian through the wilds beyond Moose-
head Lake to Chesuncook, the outpost of the
lumberman's civilization. Again anticipating
summer traffic, he went down the Allegash
and East Branch in 1857 with Edward Hoar,
a journey made memorable to him by an intelligent Indian guide from whom he squeezed
the last drop of Indian lore. In the Maine
woods Thoreau came into his inheritance of

wildness; in the presence of wildness and
woodsmen more primitive than any he had
seen, he became almost humble. For although
the lumberman was indefatigable even in
those days, choking the rivers every winter
with myriads of logs, none but the hardy and
adventurous pushed up those foaming rivers,
across those wind-blown lakes, and through
those damp, primeval forests. Apparently for
the first time Thoreau beheld vast stretches of
the wildness he had always relished; and no
wonder he enumerated the trees, measured
their girth, and pictured their native environment. "The primitive wood is always and
everywhere damp and mossy," he wrote, "so
that I travelled constantly with the impression
that I was in a swamp; and only when it was
remarked that this or that tract, judging from
the quality of the timber on it, would make a
profitable clearing, was I reminded, that if
the sun was let in it would make a dry field,
like the few I had seen, at once." Near the
untrammelled slopes of Mt. Ktaadn he began
to sense the true, inmost spirit of the wild: "It
is difficult to conceive of a region uninhabited
by man. We habitually presume his presence
and influence everywhere. And yet we have
not seen pure Nature, unless we have seen her

thus vast and drear and inhuman, though in
the midst of cities. Nature was here something savage and awful, though beautiful. I
looked with awe at the ground I trod on to
see what the Powers had made there, the form
and fashion and material of their work. This
was the earth of which we have heard, made
out of Chaos and Old Night. . . . It was the
fresh and natural surface of the planet Earth,
as it was made forever and ever—to be the
dwelling of man, we say—so Nature made it
and man may use it if he can. Man was not
to be associated with it. It was Matter, vast,
terrific—not his Mother Earth that we have
heard of, not for him to tread on, or to be
buried in—no, it were being too familiar even
to let his bones lie there—the home, this, of
Necessity and Fate. There was clearly felt
the presence of a force not bound to be kind to
man. It was a place for heathenism and superstitious rites—to be inhabited by men
nearer of kin to the rocks and to wild animals
than we." It is significant that Thoreau pre-
ferred less primitive country for a permanent
residence: "A civilized man, using the word
in the ordinary sense, with his ideas and associations, must at length pine there [in the
forest], like a cultivated plant which clasps its

fibers about a crude and undissolved mass of peat."

In contact with the essence of nature, and thereby put more than ever on his mettle, Thoreau let nothing escape him. He was interested not only in the flowers, birds, and trees, although he scrutinized them and made full lists of them in the appendix. He was also absorbed in the men who traversed this country in the line of duty, enjoying their contact with it and their feeling of competency in such a wilderness.

How Thoreau envied the woodsmen! Of two lumber scouts he passed in a canoe he wrote: "I have often wished since that I was with them. They search for timber over a given section, climbing hills and often high trees to look off—explore the streams by which it is to be driven and the like—spend five or six weeks in the woods, they two alone, a hundred miles or more from any town— roaming about and sleeping on the ground where night overtakes t h e m—depending chiefly on the provisions they carry with them, although they do not decline what game they come across—and then in the fall they return and make report to their employers, determining the number of teams that will be required the following winter. Experienced men get three or four dollars a day for this work. It is a solitary and adventurous life, and comes nearest to that of the trapper of the West, perhaps. They work ever with a gun as [with] an ax, let their beards grow, and live without neighbors, not on an open plain, but far within a wilderness." Is not this the vision of a small boy dreaming of high adventure? In this book especially, Thoreau's fresh, almost innocent, enthusiasm exhilarates the reader like the cold torrent up which he climbed Ktaadn. Let us cherish it, as we cherish all that is pure.

In the same envious spirit *The Maine Woods* reports the woodcraftsmanship and customs of these rugged men of the forests. It records the details of log-camp construction, the measurements and principles of bateaux manufacture and repair, of birch-bark canoes, the science of carrying over non-navigable regions, the size of camp-fires, the science of provisions, the details of equipment and clothing, the lore of calling moose, the principles of pitching camp, curing moose-hide, lumber running, and trout fishing. Thoreau believed in men who could manage life in this environment. Especially in the last two trips, after the apprentice period of the Ktaadn expedition, Thoreau was himself remarkably competent in the woods. In the first place, he went prepared. He had absorbed the gazetteers, reports, and chronicles; for this was no holiday for him, as with the tenderfoot tourist; it was his business, requiring more industry than usual. Having studied the maps, he was prepared occasionally to set his guide right, to estimate distances more accurately than the native woodsman, and to correct errors in the contour and boundary lines. At every moment he knew where he was in relation to landmarks; those who have invaded new country may appreciate the rarity of this achievement. In the second place, Thoreau's courage and confidence in his physical resourcefulness released his mind for detailed observation of the country. Although he made no reference to his own powers, his companion on one journey reported that the Indian sometimes relinquished the helm to Thoreau in swift water and frequently asked the direction. Eager to learn by experience as well as observation, Thoreau tried his hand at bateau poling. For the Maine woods challenged his physical resources quite as much as they taxed his capacity for observation.

After the first expedition Thoreau became chiefly interested in the Indians; and, hoping to write a book on that subject, based on chance association with wandering tribes, he now determined to study them against their traditional background. What subject could fit him more neatly? "The Indians' earthly life," he said once, "was as far off from us as heaven is." Nothing in *The Maine Woods* entertains me more than Thoreau's humble questioning of the Indian guides, and his respectful chronicles of their taciturnity or their quiet skill in the woods or on the river, as though now were the golden moment in which he might learn rich truths. One who saw a drop of moose blood on a leaf many yards away, and thus knew that a wounded animal was near, excited Thoreau's admiration excessively. Indeed, such high standards had he set for them as natural men that he criticized one who abandoned the chase too early and felt thoroughly contemptuous of another who groaned and complained over an attack of the colic. On the Chesuncook trip Thoreau's guide was a young Indian, Joe Aitteon, son of the Governor, a semicivilized youth who would have seemed dull to anyone else. Perhaps Thoreau suspected the truth himself when Aitteon confessed that, unlike his ancestors, he would not think of going to the woods without provisions. Being an idealist, Thoreau conceived the good Indian as living off the woods by preference; "subsisting wholly on what the woods yielded, game, fish, berries, etc." Nevertheless, Thoreau learned many Indian words from Aitteon and their tribal meanings, watched every move he made until the Indian seems almost to have complained; and at the end of the journey he had the good fortune to meet several Indian hunters with whom he camped one night, questioning them constantly about the habits of the moose and about the derivation of Indian nouns.

On the third trip Thoreau engaged as guide Joe Polis, "one of the aristocracy," one whom Thoreau admiringly considered a great man. Although Joe had made uncommon progress in civilization, amassing a fortune of $6,000, even journeying to Washington on official business for his tribe, he was still an expert woodsman, ready for a trip of any length with the equipment of a gun and a blanket. Few men are ever honored in literature with so complete a transcription of character and skill as Thoreau set down for this untutored

Indian guide. Joe suited Thoreau's inquisitive purpose exactly; most of the two hundred pages recording the trip expose in some fashion poor Joe Polis. One might well be alarmed to have so much of one's self reported objectively in print. But since Joe Polis frequently threw back the challenge to his inquisitor, asking him questions and testing his memory, perhaps the bargain was nearly even. And no doubt Polis maintained his self-respect by bluntly refusing certain information, avowing that "there were some things which a man did not tell even his wife." Thus, Joe Polis retained his dignity as a man; he would not be considered as a mere specimen. Thoreau's respect for him increased accordingly: "No doubt Nature has confided many things to these people," he wrote plaintively, "which are still secret to us."

Perhaps the close reader of *The Maine Woods* may begin to perceive a new quality in Thoreau, expressed in this travel essay. Lo! he begins to have Indian fancies. Halfway through the essay he appears to give off an Indian aroma himself. One cannot put one's finger on the precise spot; rather one detects a new extravagance in his impressions, more superstitious, more primitive than usual.

"It was, as usual, a damp and shaggy forest,
that Cancomgomac one, and the most you
knew about it was that on this side it stretched
toward the settlements and on that to still more
unfrequented regions. You carried so much
topography in your mind always—and sometimes it seemed to make a considerable difference whether you sat or lay nearer the settlements, or farther off, than your companions—
were the rear or the frontier man of the
camp." The acuteness of perception in that
fancy seems unalloyed Indian to me. Some
pages later, Thoreau's description of a rough,
almost impassable road, has all the quality of
an Indian legend: "If you want an exact
recipe for making such a road, take one part
Mud Pond, and dilute it with equal parts of
Umbazookskus and Apmoojenegamook; then
send a family of musquash through to locate
it, look after the grades and culverts, and finish it to their minds, and let a hurricane follow
it to do the fencing." Thoreau, thou art part
Indian thyself! More concrete evidence of
this preoccupation with Indian customs appears in his style itself. Early in this chapter
he learns from Polis the Indian name for
sheldrake, "shecorway." Immediately he
falls upon it lovingly, caressing it and append-

ing it to the English noun whenever he has the
opportunity. Before the chapter is over, however, he has appropriated it to his own use,
without apology or explanation, without ital-
ics or quotation marks: "Some shecorways,
being surprised by us, a part of them dived,"
he writes simply and henceforth becomes legitimate Indian himself! Thus has his immortality, or his reincarnation, begun on the spot.
Although we may humor him for his preju-
dices and occasional bits of ingenuous belief,
we cannot begrudge him the vividness of such
imaginative living.

The volume entitled *Excursions,* a post-
humous collection of fugitive papers, contains
several pieces in the author's best or most characteristic veins. As the result of a ten-day re-
duced-fare excursion to Canada ("the whole
expense of the journey, including the two
guide-books and a map which cost one dollar
twelve and a half cents, was twelve dollars
seventy-five cents") he wrote a hundred and
twenty-five closely packed pages entitled "A
Yankee in Canada." Here again he worked
at a high pitch to catch every truth of countryside and folk-life. He was not much im-
pressed. At St. John's: "The Canadians here,

a rather poor-looking race, clad in gray homespun which gave them the appearance of being
covered with dust, were riding about in
calaches and small one-horse carts called
charettes." So much for foreigners. As a
matter of fact, Thoreau in his old clothes and
a carriage duster, carrying his impedimenta
in a brown paper bundle, was doubtless no
more prepossessing.

Like many of his writings, the essay entitled "Walking" begins with a fanciful ety-
mology of the term and soon leaves that alluring subject for wing-beating in the thin air of
transcendentalism. "A Walk to Wachusett"
pulsates with the vivid beauties and impressions of such an excursion west from Concord.
But I like best the cool simplicity of "A Winter Walk," as fresh as the soft snow that had
just fallen, as clear as the air of that early
winter morning. No strange wonders of a
new and distant country challenge him in this
essay. No, this is Thoreau on his home
ground, conveying the joys that begin on his
snow-drifted doorstep, following the progress
of the day from morning starlight to nightfall
—to "the long winter evening around the farmer's hearth, when the thoughts of the in-
dwellers travel far abroad, and men are by

nature and necessity charitable and liberal to all creatures." Here appears one of his quiet lyrics on smoke; the other, more celebrated, appears in *Walden*. In this essay we have Thoreau at home and at his best, quite as full of affection as of curiosity; and his thinking tastes pleasantly sweet.

CHAPTER FIVE

WALDEN

EARLY in the spring of 1845 Channing wrote to Thoreau: "I see nothing for you in the earth but that field which I have christened 'Briars'; go out upon that, build yourself a hut, and there begin the grand process of devouring yourself alive. Eat yourself up; you will eat nobody else, nor anything else." Apparently Thoreau had been flirting with the same idea. Within a month he was hewing the pine timbers for his cabin at Walden Pond. For two years and two months, with only one interruption, he lived there, watching, listening, thinking, reading, and writing; and he gathered the materials for a great American book, *Walden,* incomparably the most important thing he ever accomplished. It is not only one of the few great books of American literature (as indigenous as *Leaves of Grass,* and within its field far more complete), but it is also the only book he wrote

that attracted interest in Thoreau as a thinker.
Beautiful as many passages in *A Week* may
be, and pungent as *The Maine Woods* becomes year by year, neither one disclosed
Thoreau as the poet-naturalist-philosopher—
in short, as the complete man. For beauty,
precision, richness, faith, and profundity I
think no book of our literature equals *Walden*. No book smells so much of American
soil. And if it had never been published, I
suspect that few of us would be drawn to the
quainter, more pedestrian Thoreau volumes,
nor would we suffer the eccentricities of its
author for the sake of his innate genius. Most
of Thoreau's writings endure as new aspects
of the author of *Walden;* they prove that he
was no temporary instrument of the gods, no
"sport," as the scientists word it, but a pro-
gressive thinker prepared for *Walden* by all
his past, and well-nigh emptied by its comple-
tion. In *Walden* we may enjoy the quintes-
sence of Henry Thoreau.

Being fellows of arid imagination, thoroughly perplexed by anything bold, the schol-
astics have been quick to index this volume
as "the Walden experiment," like the Brook
Farm hoax, or the Fruitlands hocus-pocus.
So convenient is it to keep everything per-

fectly regular; so reassuring to draw even the dissenters within the college wall. Having branded Thoreau as a shanty-man, the bushy-bearded James Russell Lowell denounced the "experiment" as unpractical and antisocial, with all the ceremony of handing down a judgment. Lowell's ideas on any vital subject were sonorous and windy; as a poet, professor, husband, father, and friend he was no better than a pompous gentleman. If this picturesque period in Thoreau's life were an experiment, those who object that he cheated a little in accepting home-made pies and cakes might not be as ridiculous as they seem. One has only to read a few pages of *Walden,* however, to discover that Thoreau was gratifying his love of the wild by living as close to the out-of-doors as our frail physiques make possible; he was indulging himself in the luxury of the same leisure that the plants enjoy.

Although I read *Walden* frequently with increasing relish, and accept the principles even when I scout the facts, I shall never live by choice two years and two months in a one-room cabin, nor shall I strive hard to reduce my table-board expenses. One need not swallow the camel. Those who find *Walden* packed with truth need not be reduced to living eight months on $8.74 for their nourishment; moreover, they may marry if they find celibacy a bore. For even in his economy Thoreau was unwittingly the poet, and his supreme message, if one may use that clerical term, was merely the enjoyment of life. "Rise free from care before the dawn, and seek adventures." Here was no system of economy and philosophy; systems include only experienced joys. And no one knew better than Henry Thoreau that the wise man finds happiness, not in perfectibility, but in progress toward perfectibility. Thank God each day is past. When tomorrow comes with its array of delights, we shall be the better prepared.

Although Thoreau divided his subject matter between economics, philosophy, and nature fairly equally, leavening the whole lump with pawky humor, the poetry and the fun of the adventure remain the dominant characteristics of *Walden*. Viewing himself from every side, he was delighted with his role of hermit; the comments of passers-by on the road, wafted to his ears on the woodland wind, filled him with perverse pride: "Sometimes the man in the field heard more of the travellers' gossip and comment than was meant for his ear: 'Beans so late! peas so late!' for I continued to plant when others had begun to hoe—the ministerial husbandman had not suspected it. . . . 'Does he *live* there?' asks the black bonnet of the gray coat." Playing the part of the self-appointed pioneer, he dramatized himself into various situations; and like the true pioneer he built his own house, mixed his own mortar, brought sand across the pond in his boat, skated home with the firewood on his shoulder, played at housekeeping; and, to bring himself into the proper tradition, guided his simple tasks by noble books from the past. For even his bread he mixed "according to the recipe which Marcus Porcius Cato gave about two centuries before Christ." As he lived there he enjoyed to the absolute limit the release from all social restraints; in everything he undertook he strove to wring out the last drop of ultimate satisfaction. Consider, for example, his minute description of washing the floor with water from the pond, or his experiments with water-soaked pitch-pine logs on the hearth, or his pride in knowing how to wedge the ax-head or how to recover an ax that had fallen through a hole in the ice. I know no better instance of this curiosity about every natural fact, of this passionate interest in every commonplace detail, than his account of plastering the house: "In lathing I was pleased to be able to send home each nail with a single blow of the hammer, and it was my ambition to transfer the plaster from the board to the wall neatly and rapidly. . . . I admired anew the economy and convenience of plastering, which so effectually shuts out the cold and takes a handsome finish, and I learned the various casualties to which a plasterer is liable. I was surprised to see how thirsty the bricks were which drank up all the moisture in my plaster before I had smoothed it, and how many pailfuls of water it takes to christen a new hearth. I had the previous winter made a small quantity of lime by burning the shells of the Unio fluviatilis, which our river affords, for the sake of the experiment; so that I knew where my materials came from. I might have got good limestone within a mile or two and burned it myself, if I had cared to do so." The wonder is that he did not; he always took pride in ignoring the middleman.

Constructed according to this principle and inhabited by this "expert in home-cosmography," the house soon achieved that apotheosis of all building—relation to environment.

The house belonged where it was and to whom
it sheltered. Mice nested beneath the floor; a
hare wintered there; squirrels ran over the
wood-pile; once a red fox looked in at the
window. "The phœbe . . . looked in at my
door and window to see if my house was
cavern-like enough for her, sustaining herself
on humming wings with clinched talons, as if
she were held by the air, while she surveyed
the premises." Loons and ducks dropped into
the pond; wild geese honked across the sky.
Owls, whippoorwills, and frogs talked by
night. The sensuous pleasure of fishing he occasionally enhanced by pursuing his craft at
night, making a fire close to the water's edge
—"and when we had done, far in the night,
threw the burning brands high into the
air like skyrockets, which, coming down into
the pond, were quenched with a loud hissing,
and we were suddenly groping in total dark-
ness." Can the literature of fishing match the
lyric beauty of his record of moonlight
angling? "Sometimes, after staying in a village parlor till the family had all retired, I
have returned to the woods, and, partly with
a view to the next day's dinner, spent the
hours of midnight fishing from a boat by
moonlight, serenaded by owls and foxes, and

hearing, from time to time, the creaking note of some unknown bird close at hand. Those experiences were very memorable and valuable to me—anchored in forty feet of water, and twenty or thirty rods from the shore, surrounded sometimes by thousands of small perch and shiners, dimpling the surface with their tails in the moonlight, and communicating by a long flaxen line with the mysterious nocturnal fishes which had their dwelling forty feet below, or sometimes dragging sixty feet of line about the pond as I drifted in the gentle night breeze, now and then feeling a slight vibration along it, indicative of some life prowling about its extremity, of dull uncertain blundering purpose there, and slow to make up its mind. At length you slowly raise, pulling hand over hand, some horned pout squeaking and squirming to the upper air. It was very queer, especially in the dark nights, when your thoughts had wandered to vast and cosmogonal themes in other spheres, to feel this faint jerk, which came to interrupt your dreams and link you to Nature again. It seemed as if I might cast my line upward into the air, as well as downward into this element, which was scarcely more dense. Thus I caught two fishes, as it were, with one hook."

A perfect paragraph! Throughout *Walden* Thoreau casts his line upward and downward into both elements of nature, with precisely this searching, confident gesture. He reports and speculates as though both processes were one.

Meanwhile Thoreau's ears were as alert as his eyes and his mind, and perhaps far more sensitive. Nothing escaped him. The routine sounds of nature that miss our ears, because they are ubiquitous, spoke clearly to his poetical fancies. Once, some years before, a college friend had given him a music box; he played it time and again, transported by the sweetness of the harmony. Suppose he had heard a symphony; he would have expired with delight! No chapter in *Walden* surpasses that on "Sounds," a complete chronicle of the music that came to his ears as he lived alone in the woods. To appreciate the sensitiveness of his hearing, and its capacity for quality as well as origin, one might well compile a list of the sounds he mentions in that one chapter, with the descriptive words applied to them. He heard the "rattle of the railroad cars," the "whistle of the locomotive," the "snort" and "scream" of the "iron horse," the "whizzing sound" of the train, the "faint, sweet . . . natural melody of the church bells at Lincoln, Acton, Bedford, and Concord," which, at sufficient distance over the woods, became "a certain vibratory hum, as if the pine needles in the horizon were the strings of a harp which it swept . . . ," the "sweet and melodious" lowing of some distant cow, the whippoorwill's "chanting vespers," the "dismal scream" of the screech owls, "the howls" and "human sobs" of the hoot owl, the "lisp" of the chickadee, the "rumbling of wagons over bridges," the "baying of dogs," the "trump of bullfrogs," the "laughing loon." Such was his appreciation of sounds. Only the rooster was wanting; and noting that, he writes: "I am not sure that I ever heard the cock-crowing from my clearing, and I thought that it might be worth the while to keep a cockerel for his music merely, as a singing bird. The note of this once wild Indian pheasant is certainly the most remarkable of any bird's and if they could be naturalized without being domesticated, it would soon become the most famous sound in our woods, surpassing the clangor of the goose and the hooting of the owl; and then imagine the cackling of the hens to fill the pauses when

their lord's clarions rested! . . . All climates
agree with brave Chanticleer. He is more indigenous even than the natives. His health is
ever good, his lungs are sound, his spirits
never flag." I quote thus at length to suggest
Thoreau's capacity for freshness: he was not
deaf to common sounds. His curiosity led
him to consider everything, the familiar as
well as the rare. And the whole scheme of his
career reinvigorates the common things at our
feet; in our rush for distance, for foreign
realms, we have nearly forgotten the beauties
of home.

All these delights of wildness and music,
however, were secondary beside Thoreau's
affection for Walden Pond. No other pond
satisfied him. Flint's Pond was much larger,
"but it is comparatively shallow, and not remarkably pure." Goose Pond was "of small
extent;" Fairhaven Bay, "an expansion of the
Concord River." White Pond at Nine Acre
Corner most nearly approached Walden, especially "since the wood-cutters and the railroad and I myself have profaned Walden,"
and perhaps also in the twentieth century,
when fire has destroyed much of Walden
woodland and picnic parties strew its banks

with debris. No mother ever watched over her child as Thoreau watched over Walden Pond; no religionist ever contemplated his deity with more wonder and admiration. Long before and ever after he lived at Walden, Thoreau visited the pond regularly in every season, measuring the height of the water, recording the dates of the breaking up of the ice, fishing, swimming, boating, always admiring. He viewed it from every angle, from all the surrounding hills and from all points on the shore. He gazed down from his boat at the mysteries that strewed the bottom. He sounded it thoroughly with a line, mapped it completely, drew the contours of the bottom, and compared it meticulously with all the neighboring ponds. Every day it surprised him; every day the colors changed or the surface presented new aspects. A stupendous pond! To him it was remarkable for the purity of its water and the astonishing depths, "so steep that in many places a single leap will carry you into water over your head." "Successive nations perchance have drank at, admired, and fathomed it, and passed away, and still its water is green and pellucid as ever. Not an intermitting spring! Perhaps on that spring morning when Adam and Eve were

driven out of Eden, Walden Pond was already
in existence, and even then breaking up in a
gentle spring rain accompanied with mist and
a southerly wind, and covered with myriads
of ducks and geese, which had not heard of the
fall, when still such pure lakes sufficed them.
Even then it had commenced to rise and fall,
and had clarified its waters and colored them
of the hue they now wear, and obtained a
patent of Heaven to be the only Walden Pond
in the world and a distiller of celestial dews.
Who knows in how many unremembered nations' literatures this has been a Castalian
Fountain? or what nymphs presided over it in
the Golden Age? It is a gem of the first
water which Concord wears in her coronet."
So divine a pond that Thoreau fancied the
railroad men must be better for their fleeting
glimpse of it every day, this "vision of serenity
and purity." Even the rude lines of his poem
cannot quite subdue his passion for this New
England pond:

> It is no dream of mine,
> To ornament a line;
> I cannot come nearer to God and Heaven
> Than I live to Walden even.
> I am its stony shore,
> And the breeze that passes o'er;
> In the hollow of my hand

Are its water and its sand,
And its deepest resort
Lies high in my thought.

Nevertheless, even a misanthrope like Thoreau must make some accounting to society. All things are relative, as the laconic prince of stoics declared, and every action boasts some significance. Accordingly Thoreau gave a bold appearance to his boyish adventure by conjuring up an appropriately mature philosophy, and by kicking round a stuffed shirt labelled "Economy." Indeed, such a brave face did he put on in *Walden* that he launched his book with a hundred and thirty pages of extravagant abuse of our economic system, and suggested, even if he did not deliberately say so, that his adventure pointed the sure way to escape that social complexity. Most of it may be dismissed as pure truculence, as exhilarating shadow-boxing, all expressed in hyperbole in order that the mustard grain of truth may not be lost. What practical value has this introductory chapter? Primarily it reminds us again of the essentials of life; it distinguishes necessities from luxuries, and it shows us the price in life we are paying. Let us free ourselves from all encumbrances; "I had three pieces of limestone on my desk, but I was

terrified to find that they required to be dusted
daily, when the furniture of my mind was all
undusted still, and I threw them out the window in disgust. How, then, could I have a
furnished house? I would rather sit in the
open air, for no dust gathers on the grass, unless where man has broken ground." Writing
in the graphic images of everyday life (for he
was ever the parsimonious Yankee), Thoreau
describes the dangers of "progress," and the
toll they exact from us all until we become
slaves to our freedom: "And when the farmer
has got his house, he may not be the richer
but the poorer for it, and it may be the house
that has got him. As I understand it, that was
a valid objection urged by Momus against
the house which Minerva made, that she 'had
not made it movable, by which means a bad
neighborhood might be avoided'; and it may
still be urged, for our houses are such unwieldy property that we are often imprisoned
rather than housed in them; and the bad
neighborhood to be avoided is our own scurvy
selves. I know one or two families, at least,
in this town, who, for nearly a generation,
have been wishing to sell their houses in the
outskirts and move into the village, but have
not been able to accomplish it, and only death

will set them free." When a woman offered
Thoreau a mat, he declined, for he had no
spare time within or without to shake it. "It
is best," he counsels, "to avoid the beginnings
of evil." All such economy belongs in the
familiar tradition of Socrates, of mendicants,
of celibates, and of all who renounce the world
for finer achievements of the mind and spirit.
In the nobler sense we cannot begin to live
until we have thrust out the means of living.
Even the copy-books warn us that the pursuit
of riches leads straight to the grave; "most of
the luxuries, and many of the so-called com-
forts of life, are not only not indispensable,
but positive hindrances to the elevation of
mankind." True to his time and environment,
Thoreau distrusted luxuries as breeders of
sloth and indulgence. Like the Puritans, he
respected hard, determined industry, and he
martyred himself for the cause. If the facts
of his career set him apart as an individual,
the economic principles accorded with those
of his neighborhood. As his neighbors attended to their several businesses, so he strove
to drive the same sharp bargain in matters of
life. Although he writes of "Economy" in
his usual trenchant style, expressing the arid
principles of that science in pulsating images

of life, that chapter is not remarkable for originality of thought. In this sort of thinking at least, Thoreau was no pioneer.

In the practice of economy he revealed himself as intelligent and forward-looking. Nothing seemed to him more preposterous than the folly of mortgaged property. He paints its futility in garish colors. "When I consider my neighbors, the farmers of Concord, who are at least as well off as the other classes, I find that for the most part they have been toiling twenty, thirty, or forty years, that they may become the real owners of their farms, which commonly they have inherited with encumbrances, or else bought with hired money —and we may regard one third of that toil as the cost of their houses—but commonly they have not paid for them yet. It is true, the encumbrances sometimes outweigh the value of the farm, so that the farm itself becomes a great encumbrance, and still a man is found to inherit it, being well acquainted with it, as he says. On applying to the assessors, I am surprised to learn that they cannot at once name a dozen in the town who own their farms free and clear." Truly, this is bondage of the cruelest sort, to sell one's life to a piece of property. Since Thoreau's time real estate credits have expanded until 30% of the rent commonly pays merely the interest on some other person's borrowed capital.

Thoreau's economy of living at Walden Pond may be no panacea. According to his own figures his expenses for eight months were:

House $28.12½
Farm (one year)......................... 14.72½
Food (eight months)..................... 8.74
Clothing, etc. (eight months).............. 8.40¾
Oil, etc. (eight months).................. 2.00

In all $61.99¾

During the same period he earned

By sale of farm produce................... $23.44
By day labor............................ 13.34

In all $36.78

In conclusion he writes: "which subtracted from the sum of the outgoes leaves a balance of $25.21¾ on the one side—this being very nearly the means with which I started, and the measure of expenses to be incurred—and on the other, beside the leisure and independence and health thus secured, a comfortable

home for me as long as I chose to occupy it"—
a comfortable house, in fact perched on Emerson's land without charge or encumbrance to
Henry David Thoreau.

It would be idle to attempt a moral lesson
from these thrifty figures. Who wants to imi-
tate the proportions of Thoreau's life or to
dispense with the amenities of civilized comfort for the sake of a copper or two? Most
of us can scarcely avoid the problem of ground
rental as neatly as he did. But the principles
of this accounting have pertinent relation to
the methods of domestic financing in common
practice. Thoreau showed a handsome profit
on his capital investment in these first eight
months. Unlike most of his neighbors he set
up housekeeping with sufficient capital to
build his cabin, $28.12½; he was not forced
into mortgaging his adventure in advance.
At the end of the eight months he had earned
$2.90¾, or a fraction over ten per cent of his
original investment. Let us not quibble over
his spending nearly as much for clothing as
for food, despite his frequent animadversions
on that theme. A vain fop he must have been
alone there in the woods! The fact remains
that his living expenses were on a sound foun-
dation, thrifty if blatantly parsimonious; and

he might well go on occupying his "comfort-able house" and enjoying "leisure and inde-pendence and health" just as he boasted he might in the first chapter of *Walden*.

In his philosophy, a magic compound of observation and dreaming, Thoreau swept the skies. None of the stupid baggage of world-liness checked his flight. Reassured by Nature of the things most of us distrust, and likewise distrustful of the worldly things we accept as inevitable, Thoreau dared to believe in the healthiness of life, in the possibilities of man, and in the existence of God, not as a remote deity, but as an immediate impulse in daily life. "Men esteem truth remote, in the out-skirts of the system behind the farthest star, before Adam and after the last man. In eternity there is indeed something true and sublime. But all these times and places and occasions are now and here. God himself culminates in the present moment and will never be more divine in the lapse of all the ages. And we are enabled to apprehend what is sublime and noble only by the perpetual instilling and drenching of the reality that surrounds us. The universe constantly and obediently an-swers our conceptions; whether we travel fast

or slow, the track is laid for us." Here were
none of the stuffy superstitions of hell fire and
brimstone, of redemption by penance, nor of
original sin. To Thoreau, more, I think, than
to any other thinker on nature, immortality
began instantly: "God himself culminates in
the present moment." The past we need remember only for its faltering gleams of wisdom.

No doubt his philosophy (like his poetry,
of which it is a part) could not withstand too
well a scientific examination; its renunciation
of facts as inferior to truths gives it an im-
perial advantage. And we may unimagina-
tively classify some of its more conspicuous
elements: pantheism, mysticism, transcendentalism, lyricism, idealism, all nebulous uncertain terms which are positive names for
scientific doubts. Nor did Thoreau escape the
pathetic fallacy: of the ponds he says: "How
much more beautiful than our lives, how much
more transparent than our characters are they!
We never learn meanness from them." But
one essential quality in Thoreau's philosophy
is an axiom of science; i.e., the vaulting progress of life, Nature's constant working toward
health. Let us begin at the beginning, which
is Nature. Thoreau distrusted the pious abor-

tions of the religionists, the perversions of emotion into fears and direful auguries. "Our manners have been corrupted by communication with the saints," he writes somewhat perversely. "Our hymn books resound with the melodious cursing of God and enduring Him forever. One would say that even the prophets and redeemers had rather consoled the fears than confirmed the hopes of man. There is nowhere recorded a simple and irrepressible satisfaction with the gift of life, any memorable praise of God." One need not worry about the salvation of human life on these terms. In contemplating one's own spiritual deficiencies, one is, by that sign, contemplating the entire human problem. The parts are not to be separated from the whole.

Like Emerson, who reasoned from the same premises but with less practical experience, Thoreau lived by faith, expectant and prepared. Sometimes the eternal secret for which we are all striving seemed to him hidden beneath a leaf near by or in the next cove of the pond, awaiting his coming. Nothing in his philosophy is more exhilarating than this celestial confidence in the future; nothing better reveals the goodness, the essential nobility of Thoreau's character. "My instinct tells me that my head is an organ for burrowing, as some creatures use their snouts and fore-paws, and with it I would mine and burrow my way through these hills. I think that the richest vein is somewhere hereabouts; so by the divining rod and thin rising vapors I judge, and here I will begin to mine." Reading the gospel, not in bound volumes, but in boundless nature, he did not fear or doubt. *He knew*. He was a part of *it*. "Why should I feel lonely? Is not our planet in the Milky Way?" And if any uncertainties troubled his life at the pond they were personal problems —a slight terror lest he should not be fully prepared, lest by withholding himself ever so slightly from Nature he should miss a broad hint at his feet. According to our more phlegmatic standards, however, he had little to fear. By rigid discipline he had attuned himself well-nigh perfectly, so that all his senses, his body, mind, and emotions, responded to the faintest tintinnabulations. "Sympathy with the fluttering alder and poplar leaves almost takes my breath away; yet, like the lake, my serenity is rippled but not ruffled." Nor was his curiosity ever satisfied. Having been over the pond many times thoroughly, peering into every corner, and having tramped every corner

of Concord in search of its private secret, he
went again and again no less meticulously;
and he was rewarded by learning something
new. For ultimate satisfaction in life I know
of nothing more certain than Thoreau's belief
that the qualities of his happiness lay wholly
within himself. He could blame neither
people nor circumstances. Upon his success
in preparing himself depended the fullness
of the beauty and truth he received. "What
good I do, in the common sense of that word,
must be aside from my main path, and for the
most part wholly unintended. Men say, prac-
tically: Begin where you are and such as you
are, without aiming mainly to become of more
worth, and with kindness aforethought go
about doing good. If I were to preach at all in
this strain, I should say rather: Set about being good." Even those who complain of his
distrust of ordinary sociability will attest to
the sheer goodness of his character. No one
has tried harder to live a noble life.

If Thoreau's preference for *being* good to
doing good seems like selfishness, according
to social standards, his idealism gives it a
different color. He was not deterred from
striving for nobility merely because his fellows

seldom thought in those terms. Like him,
they, too, were potentially noble; they had
only to blow the dust off their brains and
sharpen their eyesight. "Man's capacities
have never been measured; nor are we to judge
what he can do by any precedent, so little has
been tried." If only people could be shaken
out of their torpor, if only they could look
across the hills; if only they would hope!
"The universe is wider than our views of it."
Thoreau envisaged an Utopia in which every
man would be living to the peak of his abil-
ities, alive in all his parts, superb in all his
manifestations, thereby taking up the slack of
universal life and extracting the last sweetness
from its essence. "Morning is when I am
awake and there is a dawn in me. Moral
reform is the effort to throw off sleep. Why
is it that men give so poor an account of their
day if they have not been slumbering? They
are not such poor calculators. If they had not
been overcome with drowsiness, they would
have performed something. The millions are
awake enough for physical labor; but only one
in a million is awake enough for effective
intellectual exertion, only one in a hundred
millions to a poetic or divine life. To be
awake is to be alive. I have never yet met a

man who was quite awake. How could I have looked him in the face?"

By the time *Walden* was about to be published, several years after he had left the pond, and he was writing a conclusion to this epochal volume, Thoreau was beginning to dignify his holiday with the term "experiment." "I learned this, at least, by my experiment," he said, "that if one advances confidently in the direction of his dreams, and endeavors to live the life which he has imagined, he will meet with a success unexpected in common hours. He will put some things behind, will pass an invisible boundary; new, universal, and more liberal laws will begin to establish themselves around and within him; or old laws will be expanded and interpreted in his favor in a more liberal sense, and he will live with the license of a higher order of beings. In proportion as he simplifies his life, the laws of the universe will appear less complex and solitude will not be solitude, nor poverty poverty, nor weakness weakness. If you have built castles in the air, your work need not be lost; that is where they should be. Now put the foundations under them."

In other words, Thoreau had had a good time camping at Walden Pond. For the

truths he expresses in this paragraph belong
no more natively to Walden Pond than to
Main Street, Concord, Massachusetts, where
Thoreau observed them for the rest of his life.
If this Walden sojourn were an experiment,
if it were an endeavor to discover the secret
of wise and happy living, I am sure Thoreau
would have recommended it to his readers.
He recommends so many other, trivial things.
But he discouraged converts: "I would not
have anyone adopt *my* mode of living on any
account; for beside that, before he has fairly
learned it, I may have found out another for
myself. I desire that there may be as many
different persons in the world as possible; but
I would have each one be very careful to find
out and pursue *his own* way, and not his
father's or his mother's or his neighbor's instead." The Walden experience was the most
congenial to Henry David Thoreau; congenial
things are the ones a man enjoys performing.
In consequence, Thoreau enjoyed his secluded,
picturesque hut squatting on the shores of the
pond that he loved passionately all his life.
While he was there he kept his Journal carefully, worked on his first volume, *A Week,*
for publication two years later, and gathered
the material for the one book that puts him

among the great writers and thinkers of the modern world. "He was a student when he came to Walden," H. S. Salt shrewdly observes; "when he returned to Concord he was a teacher." I prefer him as a student. His study worked richer magic than his teaching.

CHAPTER SIX

GLEANINGS FROM THE FIELD

WHILE most of his parsimonious neighbors were gossiping about Thoreau's scandalous wasting of time, he was regularly scratching his thoughts and observations into the pages of his Journals, as meticulously as though his fortune depended upon them. By this time most of his neighbors are charitably forgotten. But Thoreau's Journals remain one of the most precious works in American literature, lovingly designed, gloriously written, packed with ennobling thoughts, translucent descriptions of nature, and highly charged aphorisms. "Is not the poet bound to write his own biography?" he inquires. "Is there any work for him but a good journal? We do not wish to know how his imaginary hero, but how the actual hero, lived from day to day." Whether the poet is bound to write his own biography or not, Thoreau wrote his passionately and completely in his Journals—not light-minded

tittle-tattle, but the loftiest thoughts that he
could distill from the steam of the clouds or
refract from the rays of the sunshine. "The
charm of the journal," he explained to his sub-
limated reader, "must consist in a certain
greenness, though freshness, and not in maturity. Here I cannot afford to be remembering
what I said or did, my scurf cast off, but what
I am and aspire to become." "I would fain
communicate the wealth of my life to men,
would really give them what is most precious
in my gift." None of Pepys's delicious rig-
marole, but the tracings of eternity. Perhaps
not unconsciously it is Thoreau's apology for
his life. None has ever been written with so
much glow and refulgence.

Like most journals, Thoreau's had no single
purpose over the twenty-five years of its grad-
ual maturity. At first it was a catch-all for an
ambitious young writer. At one time it may
have been "a book of the seasons, each page of
which should be written in its own season and
out of doors, or in its own locality, wherever
it may be"—the warp and woof of nature, the
texture of the seasons. At least for one period
of his life he toyed with the idea of chronicling
the news of the year, transcribing in his Journals the notes and sketches he had made out of

doors in his day-book, and perhaps at last fusing all his materials into one grand Odyssey. But he never held fast to any specific design; the several thousand pages of the completed work have no unity save his devotion to nature as the source of his life. Day by day he reported the progress of the season, the details of his observations, the harmonies of views; the heat and the cold, the hum, the melody of Nature and the thoughts he caught in her overtones, all in the vivid present tense. Sometimes he beat his way feverishly into the heavens, like his own mysterious night-warbler, and brought stardust home on his brownish wings. Of all his own records of the Journals I like best this poetic fantasy, perhaps because, being mystic, it comes closest to the truth: "My Journal is that of me which would else spill over and run to waste, gleanings from the field which in action I reap. I must not live for it, but, in it, for the gods. They are my correspondent to whom daily I send off this sheet, post-paid. I am clerk in their counting-room, and at evening transfer the account from day-book to ledger. It is a leaf which hangs over my head in the path. I bend the twig, and write my prayers on it; then, letting it go, the bough springs up and shows the scrawl to heaven; as if it were not kept shut in my desk, but were as public a leaf as any in nature. It is papyrus by the river-side, it is vellum in the pastures, it is parchment on the hills. . . . Like the seer leaves in yonder vase, these have been gathered far and wide. Upland and lowland, forest and field, have been ransacked."

Having taken holy orders for Infinity he strove always to look through nature to the ethereal blue of the beyond, taking facts "out of Nature into spirit" like the supernatural poet. "The intellect should never speak," he affirmed. "It does not utter a natural sound." Walking the fields methodically, he did not glean facts but meanings, and he struggled to cast off his experience and to look at Nature with innocent eyes until the birds "sang as freshly as if it had been the first morning of creation, and had for background to their song an untrodden wilderness stretching through many a Carolina and Mexico of the soul." If he had not succeeded occasionally, this divine aspiration might have been the pose of a fool. Every bond-holder knows that the present is real. But in rare moments Thoreau did achieve that innocence of the soul by which a simple fact repeated the dawn of the world.

Once, writing of the first bluebird, he caught that magic freshness; he stained his Journals with the true pigments of the out-of-doors: "His most serene Birdship! His soft warble melts in the ear as the snow is melting in the valleys around. The bluebird comes, and with his warble drills the ice, and sets free the rivers and ponds and frozen ground. As the sand flows down the slopes a little way, assuming the forms of foliage when the frost comes out of the ground, so this little rill of melody flows a short way down the concave of the sky." As if the slow wheel of Nature had rested a moment to let Thoreau copy the full picture down!

Studying the face of Nature, he observed "in all ages and nations . . . a leaning towards a right state of things." Do not fret about seeking adventure, but rather follow your own genius; it will not lead you astray. "Go not so far out of your way for a truer life, keep strictly onward in that path which your genius points out, do the things which lie nearest to you, but which are difficult to do, live a purer, a more thoughtful and laborious life, more true to your friends and neighbors, more noble and magnanimous, and that will be better than a wild walk. To live in relations of truth and sincerity with men is to dwell in a frontier country. What a wild and unfrequented wilderness that would be!" "And this is the art of living, too, to leave our life in a condition to go alone, and not to require a constant supervision." "We can only live healthily the life the gods assign us. I must receive my life as passively as the willow leaf that flutters over the brook. I must not be for myself, but God's work, and that is always good. . . . I feel as if I could at any time resign my life and the responsibility into God's hands and become as innocent and free from care as a plant or stone." When he returned home after the day's excursion, his thoughts were thus sublime and ideal. "Drifting in a sultry day on the sluggish waters of the pond," he confessed, "I almost cease to live, and begin to be."

As the sole custodian of natural property in Concord Thoreau's daily responsibilities were stupendous. The Journals fully account for his time. No mincing afternoon walk sufficed; it was, as he proved, a task that sometimes brought him out of doors at dawn and kept him abroad in the fields until midnight. Like old Melvin, the chopper and choreman, he had his traps to attend; jobs that required daily observation through the height of the season; mysteries to run down, and sometimes false rumors to investigate carefully, so that the records might not be wrong. Once late in January "the rumor went that a flock of geese had been seen flying over Concord. . . . I traced it to Minott, and yet I was compelled to doubt. . . . I made haste to him, his reputation was at stake. . . . Suddenly the truth flashed on me, and I *remembered* that within a week I had heard of a box at the tavern which had come by railroad express containing three wild geese. . . . The April-like morning had excited one so that he honked, and Minott's reputation acquired new luster."

Sometimes a base layman held priceless information for personal exploitation, thus impeding the swift transaction of Nature's business. Once there was a pretty state of affairs indeed when George Melvin would not tell where he found Azalea nudiflora. Thoreau's sister had brought home a flower from Mrs. Brooks's, who in turn whispered that her son had it of George Melvin. Alarums and confusions. Through several other reliable sources Thoreau traced the villainy straight to Melvin. There was no doubt about it!

Thoreau boldly went to the root of the evil,
authoritative as a warden. "Apparently he
had been drinking and was just getting over
it. At first he was a little shy about telling me
where the azalea grew; but I saw that I
should get it out of him." Alas! Melvin was
shamefully reluctant. He dilly-dallied. He
threw out wrong scents. He lied. He tried
to divert Thoreau's attention. "Well, I told
him," Thoreau says, "he had better tell me
where it was; I was a botanist, and ought to
know." For some time the argument waxed
hot and broad, involving a neighbor, irrele-
vant matters—a pair of geese and a large
brood of black ducks—and a scandalous loss
of time. But finally the aggressive forces of
righteousness prevailed: "Melvin and I and
his dog went on down the brook, and crossed
the Assabet in his boat, and he conducted me
to where the Azalea nudiflora grew." Let no
one presume to withhold vital facts! Let no
scurvy mortal stand in the way! Most of the
neighbors were willing deputies in his service: they brought him hawks and ducks to
measure and record, and they passed on whatever news they picked up on the way.

Although the business was exacting, frequently it could be attended with boyish fun,

such as trying the new bending ice up the
river, or paddling languidly on a summer evening. Walking was not for gentlemen with
starched linen and glossy shoes ; but sometimes
a hard tramp across lots all day with Channing was good sport with no relaxation of
vigilance. In wading across a thick swamp
there was satisfaction in steering only by the
sun, watching the direction of shadows, and
coming out on the far side according to plans
made by the map. Sometimes the business
might be legitimately turned to personal gain.
In the autumn Thoreau picked up firewood
along the river banks, paddled his cargo three
miles home, brought it to the house on his
back, and split it by the woodshed. "Each
stick I deal with has a history, and I read it
as I am handling it, and last of all, I remember my adventures in getting it, while it is
burning in the winter evening. This is the
most interesting part of its history. When I
am splitting it, I study the effects of water on
it, and, if it is a stump, the curiously winding
grain by which it separates into so many
prongs, how to take advantage of its grain,
and split it most easily. I find that a dry oak
stump will split most easily in the direction of
its diameter, not at right angles with it, or

along its circles of growth. I got out some good knees for a boat. Thus one half the value of my wood is enjoyed before it is housed, and the other half is equal to the whole value of an equal quantity of the wood which I buy." The plan had thrifty virtues; it was economically sound. Big business could have done no better.

In the summer the business was particularly sweet and agreeable. True to the season, Thoreau gave himself up to lazy pleasures out of doors under fair and balmy Concord skies. Somewhere up the Assabet he bathed naked in a secluded pool on hot afternoons. Putting on his straw hat as protection against the blazing sun, he used to wade up the river, still naked, looking for some new fish or frog phenomena in the humid shadows. Once on a river bank he discovered a painted tortoise laying eggs. It was rare luck; only the faithful see such things. Devoting the afternoon to this new wonder, he breathlessly watched the whole process, transcribed the incident in full, and three months later he completed his records by returning to learn the results. By getting up at 3:30 one morning, sailing up river in the opaque fog to Nashawtuck, and climbing the hill, he brought home a full report of sounds,

sights, and smells in the eerie land of islands
that poked above the mist into the fresh world
of the sun. "Men will go further," he says
sententiously, "and pay more to see a tawdry
picture on canvas, a poor, painted scene, than
to behold the fairest or grandest scene that
nature ever displayed in their immediate vi-
cinity, although they may never have seen it
in their lives."

At night, everything was as strange as
though it had never been known before—the
soft black shadows proved "that it was neces-
sary to see objects by moonlight as well as by
sunlight to get a notion of them"; "sound is
not so fugacious"; the air currents surpris-
ingly agreeable; the crickets, the whippoorwills, the night-hawk, and the baffling, elusive
"night-warbler breaking out as in his dreams,"
the wood thrush singing in "a heroic age with
which no event in the village can be contemporary." By moonlight water became more
"valuable." What a lyric Thoreau composed
of Walden Pond by moonlight! "Standing
up close to the shore and nearer the rippled
surface, I saw the reflections of the moon slid-
ing down the watery concave, like so many
lustrous burnished coins poured from a bag
with inexhaustible lavishness, and the lambent

flames on the surface were much multiplied, seeming to slide along a few inches with each wave before they were extinguished; and I saw from farther and farther off, they gradually merged in the general sheen, which in fact was made up of a myriad little mirrors reflecting the disk of the moon with equal brightness to an eye rightly placed." Moonlight and water! Thoreau did not describe them as a static quantity. In the verbal ripple and lapping of this passage he recaptured the motion of light with true scientific knowledge of its structure and with love of its rhythmic beauty.

In his "better hours" he was "conscious of the influx of a serene and unquestionable wisdom" because, like a Hindoo sage, he did not resist Nature. During long, soaking rains he could lie drenched on the ground to drain the elixir of this watery refreshment as the buds did. In an autumnal northeast rainstorm he once sailed "up the river as far as Hubbard's second grove in order to share the general commotion and excitement of the elements, wind and waves and rain. . . . I sailed swiftly, standing up and tipping my boat to make it keel on its side, though at first it was hard to keep off a lee shore. It was exciting to feel myself tossed by the dark waves, and hear them surge about me. The reign of water now begins, and how it gambols and revels! waves are its leaves, foam its blossoms. How they run and leap in great droves, deriving new excitement from each other!"

By the time he was forty he knew all the natural laws of Concord so thoroughly and the majestic flow of the seasons so intimately that he dared to identify himself with Nature, grateful in his bondage. "Almost I believe the Concord would not rise and overflow its banks again were I not here," he confesses in the Journals. "After a while I learn what my moods and seasons are. I would have nothing subtracted, I can imagine nothing added. My moods are thus periodical, not two days in the year alike: the perfect correspondence of nature with man, so that he is at home in her!" Five years later the Concord did rise and overflow his banks when he was not there. But did it? Is not the best part of Thoreau there yet? rising with the toss of the waves—blazing on every page of the Journals?

CHAPTER SEVEN

"A MAN OF IDEAS AND PRINCIPLES"

ALTHOUGH Thoreau often seemed stoical, boorish, and provincial, at least according to the popular standards of social man, those who read him closely see overwhelming evidence of his geniality—not the innocuous give-and-take of the loungers at the cracker-barrel, but the urbane wisdom of the thinker. If you ask him for light nonsense or flippant pitter-patter, you will find him austere and perhaps needlessly censorious. Within the limits he carefully marked as boundaries of his life he is mellow, humorous, and delightfully sly. So sly is his humor, in fact, so native in quality and so neatly woven into his thinking, that we often miss it completely. In its reserve it is plainly Yankee. So much so that one jocular Yankee thought *Walden* was intended as a capital satire and joke, and accordingly snickered all through it with delight! In essence his humor is a matter of

proportion, of over- and under-statement—
much in vogue among the fleet wits of this day
—in treating small matters as great, and great
as small. Throughout *Walden,* for instance,
he insists upon treating the details of his sojourn like those of the gods of Troy. Buying
a board shanty from an Irishman for $4.25,
his grave terms echo those of the dealer in
large country estates: "I to pay four dollars
and twenty-five cents tonight, he to vacate at
five tomorrow morning, selling to nobody else
meanwhile: I to take possession at six. It
were well, he said, to be there early, and an-
ticipate certain indistinct but wholly unjust
claims on the score of ground rent and fuel."
Like the Yankee trader he writes of his
townsmen whose "misfortune it is to have inherited farms, houses, barns, cattle, and farm-
ing tools," for they have got only a gold brick:
"How many a poor immortal soul have I met
well-nigh crushed under its load, creeping
down the road of life pushing before it a barn
seventy-five feet by forty, its Augean stables
never cleansed, and one hundred acres of land,
tillage, mowing, pasture and wood-lot!" "Furniture!" he exclaims later on, "Thank God I
can sit and I can stand without the aid of a
furniture warehouse."

How he loved to turn a bargain over and over in his mind, viewing it from all angles! "The nearest that I came to actual possession was when I bought the Hallowell place, and had begun to sort my seeds, and collected materials with which to make a wheelbarrow to carry it off with; but before the owner gave me a deed of it, his wife—every man has such a wife—changed her mind and wished to keep it, and he offered me ten dollars to release him. Now, to speak the truth, I had but ten cents in the world, and it surpassed my arithmetic to tell if I was that man who had ten cents, or who had a farm, or ten dollars, or all together. However, I let him keep the ten dollars and the farm, too, for I had carried it far enough; or, rather, to be generous, I sold him the farm for just what I gave for it, and, as he was not a rich man, made him a present of ten dollars, and still had my ten cents and seeds, and materials for a wheelbarrow left. I found thus that I had been a rich man without any damage to my poverty." Describing Walden Pond he used all the vast terminology of a vast ocean. He conceived the steam locomotive as an iron horse making the hills "echo with his snort like thunder, shaking the earth with his feet, and breathing fire and smoke from his nostrils," and at evening, "I hear him in his stable blowing off the superfluous energy of the day, that he may calm his nerves and cool his liver and brain for a few hours of iron slumber." Nor could he resist a trifling play on words: "Surely the railroad is as broad as it is long." He was forever playing with words, taking them apart, attributing strange meanings to them, and, like a prestidigitator, pulling out a queer object from his trick hat at last.

Something of an iconoclast as well, he made sport of his neighbors in withering irony. No wonder they protested by treating him as scornfully as their humiliating position demanded. His ridicule of silly, vapid, spuriously romantic novels cuts to the quick. Like the iconoclasts of the twentieth century he could ridicule by the familiar method of cataloging stale conventionalities, as of the newspaper foreign letter: "As for Spain, for instance, if you know how to throw in Don Carlos, and the Infanta, and Don Pedro and Seville and Granada, from time to time in the right proportions—they may have changed the names a little since I saw the papers—and serve up a bullfight when other entertainments fail, it will be true to the letter, and give us as

good an idea of the exact state or ruin of things
in Spain as the most succinct and lurid reports
under this head in the newspapers: and as for
England, almost the last significant scrap of
news from that quarter was the revolution of
1649; and if you have learned the history of
her crops for an average year, you never need
tend to that again."

None of these quotations, in fact no quotations detached from their context, can quite
indicate how Thoreau perceived the general,
perennial joke of our manner of living. In
our relaxed moments, away from the office,
most of us take that point of view now and
then. To what purpose is this impatient,
elbow-shoving scramble day by day, this
worry lest someone be running faster; and
why do none of us ever quite touch the goal?
Taking the same drum-fire tempo for our
playtime, we rush around town or to the seaside resorts, always in crowds, late into the
night, until we are never quite rested or quite
satisfied. Even in the small town of Concord
in the last century Thoreau understood this
most preposterous of the human foibles; and
when he was not shouting: "Simplicity, simplicity, simplicity," he made mordant sport
of his neighbors. Although this may not be

his most inspiring, nor his most skilful, literary method, it is not the stagnant stoicism of Marcus Aurelius.

Some of the traits for which he was unceremoniously dismissed by his contemporaries were merely fancies that grew upon him. No one regretted more than he did his fondness for paradox, and eccentric, overly bold statement, at times almost insupportable in conversation—all symptoms of self-consciousness. Alas! one who was so drilled in the manners of the woods could not behave well in society. He understood that, too. In the Journal he confesses: "My companion tempts me to certain licenses of speech; i.e., to reckless and sweeping expressions which I am wont to regret that I have used. I find that I have used more harsh, extravagant, and cynical expressions concerning mankind and individuals than I intended. I find it difficult to make to him a sufficiently moderate statement. I think it is because I have not his sympathy in my sober and constant view. He asks for a paradox, an eccentric statement, and too often I give it to him." The legend of his extreme provinciality grew in some such fashion. Many believe that Thoreau mistook Concord

for the entire universe. Whatever he may
have said whimsically upon that subject, and
however much his manner of life may seem
to support that contention, the broadness, the
universality of his interests, suggest the contrary. Does he not take pride in being an
inhabitant of the Milky Way? His pages
reek with facts about Russia, India, France,
and all the world, facts learned from broad
and eager reading. He knew history in the
most universal meaning of that science.
Upon several occasions, moreover, he confessed himself glad to know that the world
was large, and all true to the same principles:
"Would it not be worth while to discover nature in Milton? be native to the universe? I,
too, love Concord best, but I am glad when I
discover, in oceans and wildernesses far away,
the material of a million Concords." He
loved the most pungent reminders of far-off
places: "I am refreshed and expanded when
the freight train rattles past me and I smell
the stores which go dispensing their odors all
the way from Long Wharf to Lake Cham-
plain, reminding me of foreign parts, of coral
reefs, and Indian oceans, and tropical climes,
and the extent of the globe." In the "Conclusion" to *Walden* he sighs with relief:

"Thank Heaven, here is not all the world."
His apparent provinciality was but a part of
his principle to look closely for the treasures
within arms' reach.

In principle Concord represented the universe: the seasons brought universal changes;
the natural phenomena in variety and in development indicated the universal, divine
guidance. One who sought universal understanding, therefore, must first drink the waters
at home. Let us not travel, he would say,
until we are prepared, until by working at
home we have learned what to look for.
"Only that travelling is good which reveals to
me the value of home and enables me to enjoy
it better." Like Emerson, he saw no virtue in
the mere motions of travelling; the super-
ficialities of foreign languages, foreign customs and enterprises seemed to him less important than the profound truths common all
through the universe. Even in Paris the natives eat and sleep. One need not be provincial to keep these things in mind.

As every page he wrote suggests, one of
Thoreau's tenderest traits was his love of Concord, his "genius for staying at home." No
man has represented the idea *Concord* so perfectly; what Pepys was to London, Thoreau

was to Concord, and vastly more. He was indigenous; he flourished there; he knew the
seasons and guided his flow of sap accordingly.
Tutoring in New York at the age of twenty-
six, he wrote home longingly: "I have hardly
begun to live on Staten Island yet; but like
the man who, when forbidden to tread on
English ground, carried Scottish ground in
his boots, I carry Concord ground in my boots
and in my hat—and am I not made of Concord dust? I cannot realize that it is the roar
of the sea I hear now, and not the wind in
Walden woods. I find more of Concord, after
all, in the prospect of the sea, beyond Sandy
Hook, than in the fields and woods." Shall
we condemn him for this gentle nostalgia, for
the homing instinct of the carrier pigeon?
Wherever he was, he once boasted, in woods
or in cities miles from home, he could immediately face his own doorstep without consult-
ing a compass—so powerful was the homeward pull. "I am so wedded to my way of
spending a day—require such broad margins
of leisure, and such a complete wardrobe of
old clothes—that I am ill fitted for going
abroad. Pleasant it is sometimes to sit at
home, on a single egg all day, in your own
nest, though it may prove at last to be an egg

of chalk. The old coat that I wear is Concord; it is my morning robe and study-gown, my walking dress and suit of ceremony, and my nightgown after all. Cleave to the simplest ever. Home — home — home. *Cars* sound like *cares* to me." Not that Thoreau was a strong communal force in Concord. But more than anyone else he knew and loved Concord for itself as a bright speck in the solar system, keeping the accounts that everyone else neglected: "So many autumn, ay, and winter days, spent outside the town, trying to hear what was in the wind, to hear and carry it express! I well-nigh sunk all my capital in it, and lost my breath into the bargain, running in the face of it. If it had concerned either of the political parties, depend upon it, it would have appeared in the Gazette with the earliest intelligence. At other times, watching from the observatory of some cliff or tree to telegraph any new arrival; or waiting at evening on the hilltops for the sky to fall, that I might catch something, though I never caught much, and that, manna-wise, would dissolve again in the sun."

For the political life of Concord, or the political life of any part of the world, he had only contempt; to him it was not a true record of human existence. "It appears to me," he wrote in the Journal, "that those things which most engage the daily attention of men, as politics, for instance, are, it is true, vital functions of human society, but should be unconsciously performed like the vital functions of the natural body." Not believing in the state's passive approval of slavery, he never voted, nor paid poll tax; and was once imprisoned overnight for that offense. (The picturesque story of Emerson's greeting Thoreau in jail with: "Henry, why are you here?" and Thoreau's replying: "Waldo, why are you not here?" is not true, like most picturesque anecdotes of Thoreau.) Had he been a man of fiery temperament, he would have been an agitator for active revolution. "I cannot for an instant recognize that political organization as *my* government which is the *slaves'* government also. . . . When a sixth of the population of a nation which has undertaken to be a refuge of liberty are slaves . . . I think it is not too soon for an honest man to rebel and revolutionize." In his early life Thoreau held opinions about political government that were heretic by reason of their idealistic common sense. Occasionally when

circumstances required expression, he wrote
or spoke in no equivocal terms. And upon
such occasions his truculence did little honor
to the foster-child of Nature.

In 1859, however, the political fate of one
man in whom he believed drew him beyond
himself to a civil nobility quite equal to the
loftiness of his general principles of life.
Courageously championing John Brown,
while others counselled discretion, Thoreau
made one of the most beautiful, thoroughly
impassioned speeches of his life. To read "A
Plea for John Brown," after reading "Civil
Disobedience" or "Slavery in Massachusetts"
is to realize how keenly Thoreau felt upon
that sensational political topic. For this moment he abandoned the pusillanimous rhetoric
of his social addresses, and spoke with the
same heavily charged sincerity characteristic
of his pæans of nature: "A man of rare common sense and directness of speech, as of
action; a transcendentalist above all, a man
of ideas and principles—that was what distinguished him. Not yielding to a whim
or transient impulse but carrying out the
purpose of life"; "I rejoice that I live in
this age, that I am his contemporary"; "I do
not wish to kill nor to be killed, but I can

foresee circumstances in which both these things would be unavoidable"; "I plead not for his life, but for his character—his immortal life; and so it becomes your cause wholly, and is not his in the least." I should like to have been present when those words were spoken. After those days, fraught with hysterical misunderstanding and frantic recourse to merely written law, Thoreau never lapsed into the surly complacence of his former days.

Already his health was failing rapidly; he had less than three years more to live. But so closely did he identify himself with the affairs of the nation that, like Emerson, he forgot his pacificism in the belief that the Civil War was regenerating America. Although one sees now very clearly the mere opportunism of that belief, one must enjoy the spectacle of such evidence of impassioned feeling, and forgive an idealist for such a human peccadillo. In spite of himself Thoreau became a member of society; and, ironically enough, upon the same idealistic principles by which he had previously condemned it. Thus was the world, human and natural, grander than he had imagined. There were, in fine, more things in heaven and earth than were dreamed of in his philosophy.

Under the circumstances we may legitimately inquire whether his philosophy succeeded; i.e., whether he won happiness in the
life scheme he devised. Surely, by stubborn
persistence and sometimes by ruthlessness, he
pointed his career deliberately in the direction
of happiness. But if the answer cannot be a
clear affirmative, neither can it be a firm nega-
tive. Like everyone else he had his moments
of ecstasy, when his scheme seemed to be
working; and he was likewise uncertain at
times. His letter to Harrison Blake in 1849
indicates appropriate satisfaction in his determination to leave society behind: "I am aston-
ished at the wonderful retirement through
which I move, rarely meeting a man in these
excursions, never seeing one similarly engaged, unless it be my companion when I
have one. I cannot help feeling that, of all
the human inhabitants of nature hereabouts,
only we two have leisure to admire and enjoy
our inheritance." More to the point is another letter to the same admirer in 1856: "I
am grateful for what I am and have. My
thanksgiving is perpetual. It is surprising
how contented one can be with nothing definite—only a sense of existence. Well, anything
for variety. I am ready to try this for the

next ten thousand years, and exhaust it. How
sweet to think of! my extremities well charred
and my intellectual part, too, so that there is
no danger of worm or rot for a long while.
My breath is sweet to me. Oh how I laugh
when I think of my vague, indefinite riches!
No run on my bank can drain it, for my wealth
is not possession, but enjoyment."

However, we must not take a man's word
for his own happiness, no matter how sin-
cerely it is offered. Does any man know?
What he knows rather is the high-road to happiness whither he hopes to climb, enjoying the
prospects on the way. When Thoreau found
himself able to travel the remote trail that he
believed led to Nirvana, he was by that sign
contented and confident. But his frequent
protestations of happiness, although lucid in
style, imply contrast with times when another
mood sat upon him. For how can a man know
himself to be happy unless unhappiness has
set a standard for comparison?

Most of Thoreau's unhappiness, one as-
sumes, came from the human rather than the
natural elements of life. The truth is that he
was never able to renounce society completely.
All his life he resisted it, and justified his distrust on intellectual grounds. How passion-

ately he summons evidence to expose its igno-
bility! His zeal almost betrays him. His
militancy on that subject denied him personal
associations that were by no means unworthy
and might even have helped him along the
remote path he chose to travel. Able to appreciate only simplicity in men, the dominant
trait of John Brown, Walt Whitman, and the
ignorant out-door men whom he celebrated in
print, he lost the consolation of many cultured,
highly complicated minds that were thinking
of his own problems. Nor could one who
wrote for publication, delivered lectures, and
lived in the midst of a community, quite sepa-
rate himself from his contemporaries. Especially after he became known to numbers of
people, who asked him, not to resign his
course of life, but only to show them some of
its beauties, his reluctance must have seemed,
even to him, unworthy of himself. One who
had such tremendous capacity for enjoyment
must have had just as much for pain. The
entries in the Journal, periodically closing a
friendship he never actually abandoned,
breathe a tenderness and poignancy that
hardly conceal his anguish. The faith in the
following passage does not hide the pain of
Thoreau's vivid consciousness: "Farewell, my

friends, my path inclines to this side of the mountains, yours to that. For a long time you have appeared further and further off to me. I see that you will at length disappear altogether. For a season my path seems lonely without you. The meadows are like barren ground. The memory of me is steadily passing away from you. My path grows narrower and steeper and the night is approaching. Yet I have faith that in the infinite future new suns will rise and new plains expand before me, and I trust I shall therein encounter pilgrims who bear that same virtue that I recognized in you, who will be that very virtue that was you. I accept the everlasting and salutary law which was promulgated as much that spring when I first knew you, as this when I seem to leave you." Why, we may inquire, such insistence upon bravery and renunciation? For a man of fine impulses, like Thoreau's, the simplicities of friendship would have been more congenial. Thoreau had learned harmony from Nature to very little human purpose.

I would not imply that in a comparative sense Thoreau did not enjoy happiness: at times it was a relish of living quite beyond the common experience. When he let himself go

under the most propitious circumstances, he
tasted the highest sweets that life affords. Although his life was not perfectly harmonized,
although he made errors, chiefly in judgment,
although his understanding of the spirit surpassed his understanding of human life on
earth, his principles set him a practical ideal.
When he brought them to fruition in his daily
existence, he received the expected reward.
No one is so rash as to deny that happiness
comes from living the present moment fully,
with faith in the inevitability of the next.
"I *live* in the *present*," he avowed with em-
phasis. "I only remember the past and antici-
pate the future. I love to live." That was in
a letter. But Thoreau always rose to great
heights when he addressed the impersonality
of the Journal. Consider the almost sacred
passion in this passage: "I wish to begin this
summer well, to do something in it worthy of
it and of me, to transcend my daily routine
and that of my townsmen, to have my immortality now, in the quality of my daily life, to
pay the greatest possible price, the greatest
tax of any man in Concord, and enjoy the
most! I will give all I am for *my* nobility.
I will pay all my days for my success. I pray
that the life of this spring and summer may

ever live fair in my memory. May I dare as I have never done. May I persevere as I have never done. May I purify myself anew as with fire and water, soul and body. May my melody not be wanting to the season. May I gird myself to be a hunter of the beautiful, that naught escape me. May I attain to a greater youth never attained. I am eager to report the glory of the universe. May I be worthy to do it, to have got through with regarding human values so as not to be distracted from regarding divine values. It is reasonable that a man should be something worthier at the end of the year than he was at the beginning." Even in this ethereal avowal, be it noted, Thoreau's distrust of "human values," rather curbs the flight of his transcendental philosophy. Nevertheless, one begins to understand what his sister meant when she said: "I always thought him the most upright man I ever knew."